Diamo

A Diamond Buyer's Guide

By Dirk Rendel A.J.P. (GIA)

© Dirk Rendel 2012.

Table of Contents

Introduction

Part 1 - Diamonds 101

Chapter 1: A Brief History

What are Diamonds?

From the Mines to your Engagement Ring

Chapter 2: Anatomy of a Diamond

    The Table

    The Crown

    The Girdle

    The Pavilion

    The Culet

Chapter 3: Light Performance and Cut

Let there be Light

The Dimensions of a Diamond

Chapter 4: The Six Cs of buying Diamonds

Making the Cut

Types of Cut Techniques

The Detail is in the Cut Grade

- 'Ideal'
- 'Very Good'
- 'Good'
- 'Fair'
- 'Poor'

Chapter 5: Diamond Shapes

The Difference between a Diamond's Cut and Its Shape

The Shape of Diamonds to come

- Asscher Cut Diamonds
- Cushion Cut Diamonds
- Emerald Cut Diamonds
- Heart Cut Diamonds

Hearts and Arrows Cut Diamonds

Marquise Cut Diamonds

Oval Cut Diamonds

Princess Cut Diamonds

Pear Cut Diamonds

Radiant Cut Diamonds

Round Cut Diamonds

Trillion Cut Diamonds

Crown of Light

Chapter 6: Fancy Cut Diamonds

Baguette Cut Diamonds

Half Moon/Crescent Cut Diamonds

Trapezoid Cut Diamonds

Kite/Shield Cut Diamonds

Rose Cut Diamonds

Chapter 7: The Color of Diamonds

The D-Z Color Guide

Creating Optical Illusions

Fancy Colored Diamonds

Color Treatments

Fluorescence

Chapter 8: Clarity

As Clear as a Diamond

- Inclusions
- Blemishes
- Under the Jeweler's Loupe

Diamond Clarity Grades

Clarity Enhanced Diamonds

- Fracture Filling
- Laser Drilling

To Enhance or not to Enhance?

Chapter 9: Carats, not Carrots!

Ahh, Carats!

How Carats affect your wallet

The 'Carat Conundrum'

Chapter 10: Cost

Your Total will be...

    Reading the Rap List

    Saving towards your dream diamond

Online or In-Store

Chapter 11: Confidence & Confidence- Prove it!

Why are Certificates so Important?

Diamond Quality Reports

    Gemological Institute of America (GIA)

    American Gem Society (AGS)

    European Gemological Society (EGL USA)

    Hoge Raad Voor Diamant (HRD)

International Gemological Institute (IGI)

Part 2 - What To Expect When You're Expecting Diamonds

Chapter 12: Avoid The Traps

Diamond buying Faux Pas

Scammers & Scallywags

Chapter 13: Gift Ideas For Your Loved Ones

How To Buy Diamonds For Women

    Know Her Personality

    Look Through Her Jewelry Box

    Go Shopping With Her

    Stick To The Originals

    Listen To Your Love

    Make It A Surprise

How to Buy Diamonds for Men

    Know Your Man

    Go Shopping With Him

His Jewelry Box

Watch His Dream Car

Do A Little Data Mining

He Likes Surprises Too

Chapter 14: I've Got My Diamond, Now What?

Are You Insured?

Diamond Care Tips

Part 3 - From The Laboratory Of Victor Frankenstein

Chapter 15: Synthetic Diamonds

What are Synthetic Diamonds?

How are Synthetics Made?

What To Look For In Your Cultured Diamond

The Benefits of Cultured Diamonds

Chapter 16: Simulated Diamonds

What are Simulated Diamonds?

Simulated vs. Synthetics:

What's the Difference?

How To Spot A Simulated Diamond From A Mile Away

Synthetic, Simulated Or Au Natural:

Which Do You Prefer?

Conclusion: A Lesson Well Learned

INTRODUCTION

We all love diamonds but most of us haven't the slightest clue about how to buy them. On a desperate quest for knowledge, we search fashion and wedding magazines, watch countless advice videos on YouTube and read blogs until our head hurts.

After all that, we still haven't grasped the full meaning of what it takes to buy diamonds!

What is a Diamond's Cut? How does Clarity affect price and what does Bugs Bunny's carrot have to do with diamonds? Trying to find the right answers to so many questions can leave anyone aimlessly spinning their wheel like a confused hamster. You don't want to run the risk of choosing a rock that'll leave your Bride feeling a bit underwhelmed. Nor do you want to spend the rest of your days trapped in debt after buying 'The Rock of her Dreams.'

Don't worry. I'll help you to navigate the rough terrain of purchasing that special rock that will leave onlookers spellbound.

With lessons in Diamonds 101 and a few tips and tricks for snatching the perfect rock, you'll ensure that your Bride-to-be will embody all the exquisite elegance of a debutante dripping in delectable diamonds.

How To Buy Diamonds

PART 1 – First Steps

Before you can surf the humongous pipelines at Waimea Bay Beach, Hawaii, you have to first learn how to swim. In all my years, I've never seen a toddler suddenly get up and start running 100m races and I expect that I never will. Even the fastest runners in the world must first learn to crawl.

You too must start with baby steps. Welcome to Diamond 101. This section of the guide teaches you the basics about diamonds; you'll gain a better understanding of what they are, how they're mined and end up in pieces of jewelry.

We will take a quick glance at the structure of a diamond before delving into the depths of the all too important 'Rules of Diamond Engagement' commonly referred to as 'The Cs of Buying Diamonds'.

By the time you're finished with this section, you will feel confident enough to stroll into your local jewelry store; but wait a little while because there are still a few more tricks to learn.

Chapter 1 - A Brief History

Reggae artist, Dennis Brown, once sang about his romantic woes. In the song, *Money in My Pocket* (1978), he laments about his inability to woo a fair maiden, despite having pockets stuffed with cash and a winning personality. I'm of the opinion that if he had instead stuffed his pockets with a few diamonds, maybe his fair maiden would've stopped long enough to be won over by his charm.

Don't misunderstand me. I'm not saying that pockets full of shiny rocks are all that one needs to woo the opposite sex, but there's a reason Marilyn Monroe sang "Diamonds are a Girl's Best Friend" in *Gentlemen Prefer Blondes* (1953). In fact, diamonds are everybody's best friend, not just girls. (Sorry Fido.)

It's hardwired in our brains. Since the dawn of human civilization, mankind has always placed high value on shiny objects. Colorful feathers, glistening gems and intricate body art were all used for adornment by both sexes in the hopes of attracting a mate; a diamond was, at first, simply another shiny rock to add to the tribal necklace.

With time and the development of increasingly complex human societies, man began to see more possibilities for these hard-to-find gemstones. Add the good old fashioned economic principle of Supply &

Demand and voilà, a high priced commodity was born! Diamonds have not only become one of the ultimate signs of Wealth and Power, they are the *de facto* symbol of Love.

Pop Quiz: Do you know exactly what diamonds are or how they're made? Where are they mined and sold? If you have got quick fingers and are an expert on Google Search, you've probably figured this out already. If not, don't worry. I'll break it down.

What are Diamonds?

A geologist will tell you that they're naturally-occurring minerals of carbon. A chemist will say they're a chemically inert substance composed of carbon atoms arranged in a face-centered cubic crystal lattice, while a banker will tell you that they're the high priced stock commodity that he trades on the markets in order to buy his latest Porsche. Actually, diamonds are all of the above.

Technically, a diamond is made up of the same stuff as the lead in your pencil. No joke! But I doubt your stockbroker is about to deal in pencil point commodities anytime soon.

The difference between your HB No. 2 pencil and your engagement ring lies in the fields of Physics and Engineering. Both items are made up of carbon, but the atoms in your 'Bling' are arranged in such a manner that they're chemically inert, extremely reflective and as hard as...well...diamonds.

To find out how they're made, we have to go way back to the time before T-Rex was running around with his stumpy little claws. Long ago, pieces of the outer covering of the Earth's core, (the Mantle,) broke off and made its way up to the surface by hitching a ride on a lava flow.

Since the Mantle is under more stress and pressure than a hedge fund broker that's about to lose his bonus, the atoms within the Mantle organize themselves in a manner so as to ease the tension, thus forming a cubic crystal lattice. Once these mantle pieces (no pun intended) hit the surface, they just wait around until they're mined and used for a variety of reasons including being the centerpiece of your engagement ring.

Diamonds are usually mined from areas where ancient volcanoes once stood. These hotspots are located worldwide, with the largest deposits being found in parts of Africa, India, Australia, Russia and Canada.

More than 50% of the world's diamonds are mined in Africa but, sadly, some of the African mining countries were using the proceeds from their mines to fund wars and commit atrocities against their citizens. Diamonds from such areas are often referred to as 'Blood/Conflict Diamonds' as they not only extracted the cost of sweat from the miners for their labors, but also a high price in tears and blood.

The diamond markets worldwide try to mitigate this by imposing heavy restrictions and regulations on mining operations and general diamond sales through a set of rules known as *The Kimberley Process*.

The Kimberley Process was developed in 2000 as a means to help stop the sale and distribution of conflict diamonds worldwide by tracing and certifying a diamond's point of origin. Originally developed by a few South African diamond interests in Kimberley, South Africa, the resolution now has 76 countries as signatories and has pretty much ensured the extinction of conflict diamonds.

From the Mines to your Engagement Ring

Lastly, we come to the issue of getting diamonds from the mines to the markets. Only about 20% of all the rough diamonds mined are considered to be of high enough quality for conversion to jewelry. The rest are used for industrial purposes such as polishing optical lens or for drill bits and saw blades.

As I write this, I know there will be guys pulling the 'but Honey, it has got diamonds' excuse when they're trying to justify buying a $3000 power drill. Sorry, but it won't work.

The gem-quality rough diamonds are then sorted at sorting houses, the largest of which is the De Beers Central Selling Organization. (CSO). De Beers controls the lion's share of the worldwide diamond industry, from mining and manufacturing through to retail.

Some schools of thought believe that the De Beers' Iron Grip on the industry drives up the price of an otherwise easily sourced commodity. For some, if the markets were a bit more open, your local supermarket would stock diamonds right next to the cereal.

Let's face it; the exclusivity of diamonds is what makes them so appealing. It's hard to imagine your 'Grocery List' looking like this:

Milk, eggs, cereal, diapers and a 1.5 carat (Princess cut.)

Once they arrive at the CSO, the rough diamonds are sorted into at least 5000 different categories, priced and then sold to diamond manufacturers at auctions. These auctions or sites are very exclusive; there are only 10 Sites in any given year and bidding is reserved for a select few called Site Holders. The rejects from the Sites are then usually sold through a select few private auctions. At this stage, John Q. Public can't even dream of entering these auction houses, let alone placing a bid.

The Roughs bought by Site holders are then sent to cutting houses. Only a handful of diamond cutting houses exist; these are in Belgium (Antwerp), South Africa (Johannesburg), Israel (Tel Aviv), USA (New York), India (Bombay) and Russia. Each house has a unique cutting style and specialty.

The Cuts are then passed to the next rung of the ladder, the jewelry manufacturers and diamond wholesalers. It is at this point that John Q. Public is free to jump into the bidding mix. Jewelry manufacturers set the loose cuts in various pieces of jewelry which are then either sold directly to retailers or to the future Mr. & Mrs. John Q. Public.

Such a long transit route from the mines means that by the time a diamond gets to the ordinary consumer, its price has skyrocketed. No wonder there are so many bankers driving Porsches!

Chapter 2 - Anatomy of a Diamond

Before we can delve into the depths of buying diamonds, we've got to truly understand the lingo. Do you know what a pavilion or a facet is? How about a culet? If not, then class is in session. Welcome to the first lesson.

A diamond can be divided into five main sections, Table, Crown, Girdle, Pavilion and Culet, each of which is composed of tiny, flat surfaces called facets.

(a)The Table

A diamond's table is the single facet on the top of the stone. It is considered one of the most important sections of the diamond and with good reason. Diamonds are valued on their Brilliance and Fire. In other words, their ability to reflect and refract light. So depending on the cut, a large table, or lack thereof, will be of great importance.

Some sources refer to the width of the table as the 'Spread.' Changing the width of the table affects both properties. Too small and the diamond has as much oomph as a wet firecracker; too large and its fire goes up in flames. (Pun intended.)

(b) The Crown

All diamonds have crowns, but not all crowns have diamonds. (I know, it's a lame joke.) The Crown is the section of a diamond that sits between the Table and the Girdle and serves a very important function. While the point of a diamond is to maximize the amount of light reflected through its table, not all of the light entering the gemstone should be reflected. Some of the light is dispersed.

True Masters of the Art can create gems that appear to have all the colors of the rainbow dancing gracefully on their crowns (a diamond's fire), adding to the overall allure of the rock. A balance must be found between the height and the angle of the crown so as to achieve dispersion in many directions. You want the angles to be correct so it facilitates dispersion that can be viewed from above and the sides of the gem.

Smaller crown angles lead to dispersion that is only viewable from the top while larger angles create no dispersion at all.

(c) The Girdle

A diamond's Girdle is nothing like the one Grandma has. It is the outermost part of the diamond, the belt that joins the Crown and the Pavilion. The Girdle can appear smooth, grainy, or as a flat surface and is usually graded according to its thickness. There are eight grade levels ranging from extremely thin to extremely thick and it's not uncommon for a single diamond to have multiple girdle grades.

While the Girdle doesn't impact the overall value and sparkle of a diamond, there are a few key points to note. The ideal Girdle range is from the very thin' to thick and can affect the type of jewelry being constructed. The extremely thin works well for pendants or earrings but not for rings as they tend to chip either during the setting or the daily wear and tear that rings are often subjected to.

The thickness of the girdle also affects the overall cut of the diamond by changing the angles and positions of facets in close proximity. However, an experienced diamond cutter can adjust his cut to take this into account and, as such, minimize the impact caused by a thicker girdle.

(d) The Pavilion

Though beautiful, we aren't talking about the twin pavilions in *Place Des Vosges* in Paris. Our focus is on the section of the diamond between the Girdle and the Culet; the unsung hero of the diamond. It is often hidden in the metallic grip of the setting, but its contribution to a diamond's beauty can't be overstated.

The Pavilion's angle and height must be in perfect balance with the rest of the diamond. If the height is too much or the angle is too large, then the diamond has what is termed a 'deep cut.' Light will find more ways to flee than Steve McQueen in the movie *The Great Escape* (1963). Jewelers and diamond cutters must once again find the sweet zone to get the maximum performance.

(e) The Culet

Lastly we come to the Culet, that tiny facet at the very bottom of the diamond. Due to the diamond being glued onto a stick, the very tip of the stone chips and cutters are then forced to just make a flat facet to keep the stone symmetrical.

The Culet or Cutlet, pronounced *Kewlet*, is derived from the Latin word *culus* which means 'bottom.' A culet is also a small 14th century plate armor used to protect the buttocks during combat. While the Culet may be small, don't underestimate its value. A beautiful, perfectly cut diamond can be rendered ghastly by having a not-so-perfect culet.

If the culet is too large, it can function like a black hole in space, gobbling up photons of light bouncing around in the diamond. When viewed from the Table, you'll see a large black spot and your diamond's Brilliance and Fire will be disappointingly underwhelming. A large Culet can also make a diamond seem asymmetrical and nobody likes a wonky rock.

Fortunately, these days only a very small percentage of diamonds on the market have culets, since diamond cutting has advanced to a stage where chipping the tip of the diamond can be avoided.

Chapter 3 – Light Performance and Cut

Remember the last time you bought a car? Did you just run to the dealer and say "Gimme that one!" with nary a thought about anything else? Of course not! Even those among us burdened with the task of not having to foot the bill thought long and hard about buying our last car.

What were your thoughts? Affordability? Practicality? Do I look sexy in this car? Will the Joneses at number 22 die with envy? (Cue *evil grin*). You took your time to research the car most suited to your needs and desires. You shopped around, sought the opinion of every single solitary soul you ever added as a 'friend' on Facebook and then you asked all of *their* friends. You made sure you knew enough to feel confident walking into the dealership. What makes you think that it's any different when buying a diamond?

Let There Be Light

To talk about diamonds means that we've got to first understand its Light Performance and how this affects the price of your cut gems. You'll encounter these words repeatedly throughout this book – Brilliance, *Fire* and *Scintillation*. These terms collectively refer to a diamond's Light Performance. Learn these terms as you did your Multiplications Table in elementary school as they are crucial, need-to-know facts when searching for a great diamond.

Brilliance is a measure of a diamond's ability to reflect white light, while Fire is a measure of its ability to disperse light and create a 'Rainbow Effect.'

Does it ever seem that a gem twinkles when you move it around? Gemologists call this Scintillation.

The quality of a diamond's cut has the greatest impact on its light performance and ultimately its value. When buying a cut diamond, there are certain light performance properties to take note of. Knowing these criteria can mean the difference between a good gem and a great gem.

Brilliance

First and foremost, a diamond must have brilliance. It's the first thing that we notice. As light bounces around within the diamond, it can be channeled to follow a particular path by properly aligning the facets within. The aim is to force as much light as possible into the stone, thus creating the gem's shine or Brilliance. You want to be able to signal passing airplanes and guide boats through the morning fog with your engagement ring. A great diamond should blind you with its light, metaphorically speaking.

Fire

Any engineer will tell you that it is impossible to have a system that is 100% effective at its task. So too with diamonds; they'll never reflect 100% of the light within them. Some photons are scattered like leaves in the wind. This dispersion causes the light rays to fragment, thus creating a rainbow. The beautiful optical illusion created by the 'Rainbow Effect' adds to the overall mystique of your diamond. Ideally, you want a gem to have more fire than Tabasco.

Normal white light is actually made up of many different colors which, under the right conditions, can be dispersed. We usually observe this phenomenon in the summer after a light shower of rain. The water droplets in the air disperse light, thus creating a rainbow. If aligned correctly, the facets in a diamond can act much like water droplets in the air.

Scintillation

What good is a diamond if it doesn't sparkle? Rocks that don't dazzle when you move them around are simply not very scintillating which is a measure of a diamond's sparkle.

Contrast

Life needs its contrasts and contradictions; otherwise it would be a very boring existence. What's sweet without sour, right without wrong, black without white, diet soda without a double cheeseburger?

Our brain and eyes work by comparing things. When we look at an object, our brain forms a composite of the images from our right and left eyes which helps us to judge the distance and depth of the object. Ignoring this information usually leads to tripping over the last few steps on a flight of stairs or stubbing our toes on a rock. Don't you just hate that?

Diamonds have this too. The complex patterns of light and dark areas that are created by a gem enhance its overall brilliance. I know it sounds counter-intuitive, the shadows in the diamond make it seem brighter, but it's true. A white shirt looks whiter when it's worn with a pair of lint-free, jet-black slacks. It's just how our brains are programmed.

The Dimensions Of A Diamond

With all this in mind, it is equally important to know how the dimensions of a diamond affect its Light Performance. Think of it this way, a squat hatchback isn't as fast as a sleeker model car because the physical dimensions of the hatchback don't allow air to flow over it smoothly. High performance sports cars are designed to be more aerodynamic and ultimately faster. Besides that, sleeker cars are just sexier!

Diamonds are much like your car. If it's poorly cut, light doesn't bounce around as efficiently as it should. The rock's Light Performance, therefore, becomes inferior.

The depth of the cut plays a key role. A diamond with a deep cut will allow light to leak out, hence reducing the diamond's Brilliance, Fire and Scintillation. A diamond with a shallow cut refracts too much light and the diamond appears glassy. A glassy diamond is as priceless as a set of champagne glasses from the 99 cent store.

Chapter 4 The Six Cs of Buying Diamonds

Technically there are four Cs – Cut, Color, Clarity and Carat, but, in my opinion, there are also two other factors that are of equal importance when it comes to choosing the right diamond. These are Cost and Confidence.

Whether it's a 0.25 carat or one the size of a football, the same general rules apply when it comes to buying diamonds. Before rushing out all light-headed and starry-eyed from Cupid's arrow, really ask yourself if you know the Six C's?

Let's start with the most important of them all – Cut.

(a) Making the Cut

A diamond isn't a diamond if it doesn't shine and it won't shine if it isn't properly cut. Just like Death and Taxes, this rule is an intrinsic part of life; well, maybe just an intrinsic part of buying diamonds.

Roughs are usually cut using other diamonds (remember that the hardest stone on Earth is a diamond). Roughs refer to diamonds which have not yet been cut or treated. These are 'straight from the mines.' A rough is first mounted and cut with a saw spinning at a very high RPM. The blades of the saw are usually coated with diamond powder to give it additional cutting power.

Once the diamond is roughly cut into smaller pieces, the cutter devises a plan which will allow him/her to make additional cuts with minimal waste. Even the diamond chips are of extremely high value.

The preliminary facets of the diamond are roughed out, giving the cutter a general outline of the final stone and the best angles for various facets. The crudely cut gems are then refined by a process known as 'bruting' which involves slowly shaving the gem to the desired shape using a cast iron wheel coated with diamond powder. The angles and cut lines are very meticulously monitored using precision laser instruments.

It takes great skill and years of work to master these techniques. Let's just say, if you don't have an abundance of patience and an extremely careful eye for detail, you can give up hopes of ever joining the Diamond Cutters' Guild. Just be happy with buying the gems!

Nuremberg, Germany was the first place to have an official Diamond Cutters' Guild. The Guild, formed in 1375, developed the Point Cut system which took advantage of the diamond's natural shape. First, cutters used a chisel and mallet to achieve the overall final outline of the gem. The diamond was then subjected to bruting.

The entire project produced a stone so unrefined and dark, that diamonds were considered inferior gems. As such, their popularity was overshadowed by colored precious stones. It was simply much easier to get a beautifully refined sapphire than a quality loose diamond.

Those days have obviously changed.

(b) Types Of Cut Techniques

In general, there are techniques that are employed to develop a diamond's cut.

The *Brilliant Cut* is used to create the femme fatale pieces of the diamond world. The cone-shaped pavilion is cut deep enough to encourage lots of light reflection and we all know what that does for a diamond.

The *Step Cut* embodies visual simplicity. The diamonds created with this cut are not as bright and fiery as Brilliants, but what they lack in sparkle and shine, they make up for with unbelievable clarity and clean outlines. The technique is mainly used to create square or rectangular gems like Emeralds or Asschers. (See next section.) Step Cuts have large facets arranged in a stair/step-like manner (hence the name) which acts like a mirror.

A *Mixed Cut* is the love child of the Brilliant and Step Cuts. She has her dad's clean, sophisticated lines, but beautifully captures her mom's sparkle. The Crown is done according to dimensions of a Brilliant, while the Pavilion based on the dimensions of a Step Cut. Mixed Cuts are often used to create unique, patented diamonds.

(c) The Detail Is In The Cut Grade

Remember the dreaded school report card? If you got straight A's, you skipped as if it was Christmas morning. When your grades were horrible, you tried your hand at a few forgery techniques, none of which would fool your parents.

Much like every kid in school, diamonds receive report cards. One of the subjects they are graded on is the quality of their Cut. Cut diamonds are sorted into 5 grades, each of which is defined by the amount of light the diamond reflects.

Certifying labs like the Gemological Institute of America (GIA) and the European Gem Lab (EGL) use a certain set of criteria for grading diamond cuts. Labs generally break down their grading criteria into 3 main categories: Light Performance, Design Features and

Finish, each of which is further sub-divided according to various other requirements.

I have used these two labs as an example since they generally provide the most detailed analytical reports and are the two most popular labs worldwide. While you don't need to know all the nuances of each lab's grading scheme, it helps if you're generally acquainted with their parameters. This helps you to make a better comparison, you know, as in apples with apples.

A few of these terms should already be quite familiar to you now (Brilliance, Fire, Scintillation and Girdle size) but others may still be a bit foggy. Leakage? That sounds like really horrible medical condition, doesn't it?

Relax. A dash of Logic with a sprinkle of the Power of Deduction and you've already figured out what they are without using Google.

Leakage

Just as the name suggests, it's a measure of the amount of light that escapes or 'leaks' from the Pavilion. (See Chapter 2.)

If light can't pull a 'Houdini' and make a stealthy escape from your gemstone, then the diamond has been expertly cut. The more places where light can 'leak out' from your gem results in less Brilliance and Fire. As such, your gem will have a lower cut grade.

Weight Ratio

The Weight Ratio is a comparison of a diamond's carat weight to its diameter (girdle). A diamond with a large weight ratio is very heavy (carat weight) but very narrow (girdle). As such, the diamond is cut too deeply and light isn't efficiently reflected by the gem. A small weight ratio indicates that the diamond has a wide girdle and is as light as a feather; hence it's cut too shallow. Light is easily refracted and not reflected.

Durability

Durability is a measure of your diamond's resistance to daily wear and tear. While diamonds may be the hardest stones in the world, they are not indestructible. Even Superman wasn't very 'super' when a few Kryptonite shavings spilled on his shoulders.

If a diamond is cut too thin, it's susceptible to a few chips, scratches and bruises, especially those inflicted by other diamonds. This is why it is imperative to keep your diamond protected. (See Chapter 14 for Diamond Care Tips.)

Polish

We polish our diamonds to a sparkling shine just as we would our Mahogany furniture. Jewelers will often give a diamond a good Mr. Miyagi 'Wax-on, Wax-off' to make them sparkle and to improve the gem's Light Performance.

Polishing clears away surface crud and allows more light to enter the diamond. As a result, more light gets bounced around within the stone and, presto, your diamond has much more Brilliance and Fire.

The quality of a gem's polish is categorized into different grade levels depending on the presence of polish lines. These lines result from the machinery used to polish your diamond. A poorly done polish will leave your stone dull and horribly scarred from its fierce battle with the polish wheel.

In theory, having a diamond with an 'Excellent' polish grade is wonderful but, in reality, it may be unnecessary and a waste of money that could otherwise be spent upgrading a more noticeable feature on your diamond. In most cases, a grade of 'Good' will suffice for a diamond that has a Clarity grade of SI or VS. (See Chapter 8.) If you wish to splurge, then higher polish grade levels will suit diamonds that are considered almost flawless.

Symmetry

In a perfect world, all gems would contain perfectly aligned and shaped facets. Unfortunately, diamond cutters have bad days too and we end up with diamonds that sometimes look like they were carved up by a 12 year old. When that's the case, we make note of the rock's symmetry grade.

A diamond's *Symmetry* is a measure of how well its facets are arranged in relation to each other. Just like Polish, Symmetry also has its own grade levels. These are 'Excellent,' 'Very Good,' 'Good,' 'Fair,' 'Poor' and 'Very Poor' and it is usually stated on the gem's certificate. You should walk past diamonds that are ranked at any grade below 'Good' without batting an eye as those gems just aren't worth your time.

If you want to be more proactive in your diamond hunt, then you can judge the symmetry of your diamond yourself by grabbing a jeweler's loupe and taking a good, long look at your new rock. While you're doing that, run through this checklist of questions.

- Does the Culet and/or the Table look off-center? Are they a little too much to the left or right?

- Do the facets look strange/uneven? Are they all pointing upwards towards the table? Does it look like there are too many facets for the type of Cut?

- Do the Crown and/or the Pavilion look misaligned?

- Does the Table look uneven? Does the Crown look uneven? Are they parallel to each other?

- Are there any bulges in the Girdle?

If the stone does not live up to your standards, your desires may be better fulfilled by a different gem.

Now that you have a little background information under your belt, let's get to the good stuff – Diamond Cuts and Cut Grades.

(1) 'Ideal'

'Ideal' diamonds are designed to maximize Brilliance and Fire by reflecting almost all of the light entering the gem. These cuts tend to be round, as this shape perfectly enhances and displays the exquisite lines of the stone and falls within the ideal proportions for a diamond.

In 1919, Belgian mathematician Marcel Tolkowsky interviewed renowned diamond cutters and ordinary people on the streets of London about their jewelry preferences. He made note of which gemstones they found most appealing and why. A few miles (and probably a few pints) later, he calculated the spatial criteria for the modern Brilliant Cut.

Two of the world's leading diamond certifying labs, GIA and AGS, have refined Tolkowsky's initial calculations and developed new guidelines for a perfectly cut diamond. The proportions listed below represent the generally accepted parameters for an 'Ideal' diamond, represented as a percentage of the entire diamond.

Flawless, 'Ideal' grade diamonds are very rare. You probably have a better chance of riding a unicorn through Central Park than finding such a rock. I apologize for bursting the bubble of those among us hunting for the perfect diamond.

(2) 'Very Good'

If you have a smaller budget and still want to purchase a beautifully cut diamond, then a diamond with this cut grade may be for you. Manufacturers and mines are more likely to find gems worthy to be transformed into 'Very Good' (about 20% of all gem quality stones) than 'Ideal' gems. (3% of all gem quality stones mined worldwide.)

Gems within this cut grade reflect around 70% - 80% of the light entering the table and are among the most popular stones for jewelry pieces for the well-to-do John Q. Public. 'Very Good' gems may cost a lot of moolah but the quality of these beauties is undeniable.

(3) 'Good'

If you want to sacrifice only a hand instead of an entire arm to pay for a quality diamond, then a 'Good' diamond might do the trick. This is a perfect diamond a connoisseur on a Soda Budget can get with reasonably decent quality and, in most jewelry stores, is the lowest grade cut they stock.

(4) 'Fair'

Diamonds with a 'Fair' grade or lower usually reflect less than 60% of the light that enters the gem. 'Fair' diamonds are just a few degrees brighter than 'Poor' gems but when compared to a diamond rated as 'Good', the difference in its quality is significant.

The advantage is that because 'Fair' diamonds are much cheaper, you won't spend sleepless nights wondering how much you can get for selling your old Star Wars action figure collection.

(5) 'Poor'

I call these 'Practice Diamonds' since they're probably done by Newbies just completing the first 6 months of diamond cutting school, or cutting professionals who are having a *really* bad day. These gems reflect the least amount of light and possess the worst light performance characteristics of the lot. They often appear dull and don't possess the glimmer and allure that's usually associated with diamonds.

Most jewelry stores will not stock diamonds with a 'Poor' grade as these are not usually in demand and the profit margins on these rocks are minuscule at best. No respectable jeweler wants to ruin his reputation with inferior quality gems. Doing so would ruin his chances of selling high quality, high priced items as it inadvertently fosters customer suspicion and mistrust.

Sacrificing Brilliance, Fire, and the WOW! factor for cost is entirely up to the discretion of you, the buyer. Always remember that the Love of your Life will love you regardless of which cut grade diamond you choose.

Chapter 5 Diamond Shapes

Diamonds come in all shapes and sizes and, as such, it's important that you're up on the lingo when it comes to this aspect of diamond buying. So far, we've only begun to explore one of the Six Cs - Cut. But we can't talk about a diamond's Cut without mentioning a little about the shape of a diamond.

If your eyebrows are forming tiny wrinkles of confusion, then you must be asking 'what's the difference between a diamond's cut and its shape?' Well put it this way, two diamonds can be of the same cut but have very different shapes.

The Difference Between A Diamond's Cut And Its Shape

A diamond's Cut actually affects the value of the diamond. Gemstones are cut to maximize the reflection of light, giving it more Brilliance and Fire. On the other hand, a diamond's Shape only relates to its overall outline and is a matter of the buyer's and/or jeweler's personal choice.

Think of it like this; everybody loves a scoop of heavenly, melt-in-your-mouth vanilla ice-cream, but different people prefer it served in various ways. Some are purists and like theirs as plain as day, while others love it topped with chocolate syrup.

The quality of the ice cream hasn't changed in each scenario, but it's eaten with or without various delicious additions. Likewise, a diamond may be Pear or Heart-shaped, or even shaped to resemble your big toe but, at its core, it's still a diamond. The grade only refers to how expertly the diamond has been cut.

When the shape of a cut diamond is being determined, jewelers often take into account the setting, the type of metal and the shape of the setting on which the diamond will be mounted, as well as flaws which the diamond has. The gemstones are usually shaped in a manner to not only hide its imperfections, but also to give the piece an overall artistic flair once the diamond is mounted. The shape of the gemstone rests entirely in the hands of the jeweler.

The Shape of Diamonds to Come

While it's unlikely that you will find a big toe-shaped diamond in your local jewelry store anytime soon, there are a number of other outlines to choose from, the most popular of which are Asscher, Cushion, Emerald, Heart, Marquise, Oval, Princess, Pear, Radiant, Round, Trillion and, my favorite, the Crown of Light.

Asscher Cut Diamonds

This shape was developed by The Royal Asscher Diamond Company in 1902. Its popularity was resurrected in recent years by TV shows like *Sex and the City*. The square-shaped gem consists of 72 large facets and trimmed corners. Since this shape is created using the Step Cut technique, it tends to highlight the diamond's Clarity and Color. In this case, it is best to choose the highest grade of both possible.

The ideal Asscher diamond should have a length: width (L:W) ratio of 1.00 - 1.05 and Depth and Table percentages of 60% - 68%. But be forewarned, this shape makes gems appear smaller than they really are.

Cushion Cut Diamonds

In the days before the reliable flow of electricity, your great grandpa probably wooed your great grandma by presenting her with a Cushion diamond. This shape is often called a 'Pillow Cut' or 'Candlelight Diamond' as it was designed to be breathtakingly beautiful when viewed in the soft glow of the evening's candlelight.

Like every Step Cut diamond, this beauty features large facets which highlight the gem's Clarity and Color while giving it an air of Old World mystique. It is best to choose the highest grade Clarity and Color possible since this cut emphasizes these features.

An L:W of 1.00 - 1.05 (for a more square shaped gem) or greater than 1.15 (for a more rectangular shaped rock) is considered to be the dimensions for an ideal Cushion diamond.

Emerald Cut Diamonds

This shape is a classic example of a Step Cut diamond with its huge table and large rectangular facets.

As with all Step Cuts, this shape enhances the stone's Clarity and Color. It's wise to opt for the best of both as flaws are easier to spot than an elephant standing amongst mice. Ideal examples of this cut have an L:W of 1.30 - 1.40 and Depth and Table percentages of 58% - 69%.

Heart Cut Diamonds

Heart-shaped diamonds are created by carving a small cleft in the middle of a larger Pear-shaped diamond before smoothing out the resulting lobes. They are extremely popular on Valentines Day and are mainly used to accentuate necklaces and earrings. These gems are flatter, giving the illusion of a bigger rock which in turn leads to less Brilliance and Fire. However, the shape enhances the gem's Color and Clarity.

The apex of a Heart diamond is susceptible to damage and the Bow-tie effect is evident in Heart gems to a small extent. The Bow-tie Effect is the appearance of patterns shaped like a bow-tie within a gem. This is usually caused by misshapen or misaligned facets and is characteristic of shapes like Ovals or Marquises. Ideally, stones should have an L:W of 0.09 - 1.10 with a Depth of 58% - 65% and a Table percentage of 52% - 64%. It always pays to be mindful of the stone's Symmetry; a lopsided heart isn't very romantic.

Hearts and Arrows Cut Diamonds

A Japanese cupid developed this rare diamond cut in the 1980s. Hearts and Arrows diamonds feature 58 facets that are cut and arranged to give a pattern of hearts (when viewed from the table down) and arrows (when viewed from the face up).

Due to the arrangement of facets, a huge amount of the rough diamond is wasted during the creation of these gems, hence making them very difficult to find and making them equally brutal of John Q. Public's wallet.

Marquise Cut Diamonds

King Louis XIV was so enamored by his mistress, Marquise de Pompadour, that he commissioned a diamond in honor of her gorgeous smile. This 58 facet beauty is cut to maximize Brilliance, Fire and Scintillation, while giving the illusion of a bigger stone. Marquise diamonds look exquisite on long, slender fingers.

Ideally, Marquise diamonds should have an L:W ratio of 1.75 - 2.25. The Bow-tie effect is prevalent in this cut and the gem's sharp edges have as much durability as an ice cream sundae on a hot summer's day.

Oval Cut Diamonds

Oval diamonds were developed by L. Kaplan in the early 1960s. These 57 facet, Step- Cut diamonds accentuate long, slender fingers, but prominently feature the dreaded Bow-tie effect. Ideally, the L:W ratio of an Oval diamond should be 1.33 - 1.55 with the Total Depth of 58% - 65% and a Table percentage of 52% - 64%.

Princess Cut Diamonds

Ladies love a Princess diamond. How or why this love affair began remains a mystery. Maybe they evoke starry dreams of being a princess in an enchanted land, or it could be that this cut exquisitely accentuates feminine fingers. Who knows?

Stones with an L:W ratio of 1.00 - 1.05 and Total Depth and Table percentages of 58% - 77% are considered to be ideal examples of this shape. However, Princess diamonds have high clarity, lots of color retention and a supermodel-thin girdle which makes these stones susceptible to damage.

Pear Cut Diamonds

Pear diamonds are like fragile teardrops running down a delicate, feminine cheek. These gems offer a curious mixture of stunning Brilliance and Fire with a facade of delicacy. The ideal L:W ratio for these beauties is 1.45:1.75, but they're susceptible to the evil bow-tie effect and damage from daily wear and tear.

Radiant Cut Diamonds

The clean lines and trimmed edges of this Step-Cut variant maximize the diamond's Brilliance and Fire. Radiant diamonds, as the name suggests, produces a uniformed sparkle due to the shape and alignment of its large facets. Even though these diamonds are somewhat shallow, this is generally a better cut for masking flaws and beefing up the gem's Carat Weight; however, it also tends to retain color.

Henry Grossbard developed this cut to be less prone to chipping and cracking and as a great centerpiece for Trapezoid, Trillion and Half

Moon accent stones. An L:W ratio of 1.20-1.30 and Depth and Table percentages of 58% - 69% is an ideal example of this series.

Round Brilliant Cut Diamonds

Rounds are the most loved of all the diamond shapes as they're renowned for bringing out the Fire and Brilliance of the diamond's cut. Often nicknamed 'Brilliants,' they're generally considered to be timeless pieces - the Grace Kelly or Jackie Onassis of diamonds.

Even lower quality gems exhibit excellent Brilliance and Fire with this shape. Most of the studies used to understand the dynamics of light interaction with diamonds are done using Rounds as test subjects, and it has been found that stones with 58 facets and an L:W of 1.00-1.20 are examples of the perfect Brilliant.

Trillion Cut Diamonds

Designed by the Henry Meyer Diamond Company in 1962, Trillions are enjoying a resurgence in popularity in recent years. They're generally wide, flat and triangular, which makes the gem appear much larger than it really is.

Trillions have great Brilliance and Fire, but are notoriously difficult to mount without damage. Any flaws in the gem will stand out more than a sore thumb, so it is always best to choose stones with the highest clarity possible. A stone with Total Depth and Table percentages of 43% and an L:W ratio of 1.00 is an ideal representation of the series.

Crown of Light

As I said earlier, this is my personal favorite.

A 'Crown of Light' diamond has 90 facets, compared to 57 on a traditional 'Round Brilliant'. The extra facets replace the table of a traditional round diamond or, in other words, they're on the crown.

Visually, the 'Crown of Light' has no table and is domed. That means it catches the light from all angles and there is virtually no light leakage.

However, there is one drawback. Since some of the weight of the stone is on the crown, the diamond will appear to be a little smaller thanks to its traditional round brilliant counterpart.

So, if your goal is size and not performance, this cut isn't for you.

Chapter 6 – Fancy Cut Diamonds

Every so often, a fashion designer breaks the mold by creating unusual outfits. Diamond cutters are the fashion designers of the jewelry world, and they also envision strangely contorted beauties meant for the more esoteric of tastes.

Sometimes these designs fall by the wayside like pink leotards and shoulder pads from the 1980s. Others seem have as much fashion longevity as a string of Mikimoto pearls and are zealously gobbled up by diamond consumers.

Fancy cuts are basically gems which have been cut into non-traditional shapes like Round or Princess. They are usually variations of one or more cutting techniques (see Chapter 4) and are often done to enhance a specific feature (to give a gem more Fire than Brilliance) or help cover up flaws.

Baguette-Cut Diamonds

That delectable French morsel inspired a diamond cutter at the turn of the 20th century to design the Baguette cut. These gems were more popular in the 1920s and 1930s than boy bands were in the 1990s.

Baguette diamonds are comprised of 14 large facets which bring out the stone's clarity and color. These diamonds are mainly accent stones as they tend to carry a smaller Carat Weight (see Chapter 9). The L:W for the perfect Baguette diamond is 1.00- 1.50.

Half Moon/Crescent Cut Diamonds
The Moon has inspired many of the world's finest works of art and diamonds are no exception. This cut is usually created from Marquise diamonds and was extremely popular in the 1920s and 1930s. In fact, many of the more unusual cuts were popular during that time.

The Half Moon or 'Demilune' diamond makes a fantastic accent stone with Asscher, Princess, Radiant and Emerald diamonds while its crescent-shaped cousin fits beautifully with Oval, Round, Marquise and Cushion centerpieces. Ideally, the stones should have an L:W ratio 2.00-1.75. The stones are always offered as a pair (would you wear only one sock?) but finding a perfectly matching pair can sometimes be difficult and costly.

Trapezoid-Cut Diamonds

Rumor has it that the aerial maneuvers of trapeze artists were the inspiration behind this cut. Personally, I don't see the family resemblance, but maybe you have better eyes and a bigger imagination than I do.

The cut can be achieved using two cutting techniques. When the shape is created using the Brilliant Cut technique, it produces a beautiful stone with intricate patterns and lots of Brilliance and Fire. This makes a great accent stone for Radiant and Princess centerpieces. By using the Step Cut technique, the gem contains long, parallel facets with clean lines and amazing clarity. In this case, it's a perfect sidepiece for Emerald and Asscher diamonds. A new variation is the Crescent Trapezoid which is more suited to Oval, Cushion, Marquise and Round cuts.

Trapezoid diamonds run cheaper because they result in less wastage of the rough diamond from which they are cut.

Kite/Shield-Cut Diamonds

Kite diamonds aren't designed for flying, but they're usually embellishments for other centerpieces, earrings and pendants. Kite diamonds are an example of the Brilliant Cut technique. A Star diamond can be constructed by assembling five Kite diamonds in a star pattern.

Rose-Cut Diamonds

Rose diamonds were extremely popular between the 1500s and the 1900s. Depending on the size, these stones contain anywhere from 3-24 facets and are usually centerpieces for antique jewelry like Grandma's engagement ring. It's a bit tricky to find these beauties; you'll need to perform a thorough search of antique stores or dig through your family heirlooms. As such, expect to spend a pretty penny for Rose diamonds.

Rose cuts generally have large carat weights and, as such, they're not usually the brightest tool in the shed (See the 'Carat Conundrum.') This could account for its fall in popularity since the turn of the 20th century. In today's world of Glam, Flash and Bling, seemingly dull stones are more suited for the connoisseur of the unusual. To give these gems some spunk and shine, jewelers often place thin strips of highly reflective gold or silver foil on the back of the stone before setting it.

If your Love is a softy for the classics, then dust off Grandma's old Rose diamond engagement ring. This gesture will mean much more to her than the flashiest ring money can buy.

Chapter 7 – The Color Of Diamonds

Color, or rather the absence of it, is a highly sought after characteristic of diamonds. Jewelers seek out stones that exhibit the least amount of color, because the presence of even a tinge of hue can result in the loss of Fire and Brilliance, two characteristics that form the backbone of a perfect diamond.

However, this rule doesn't apply to Fancy Colored diamonds, where color is the stone's most desirable trait; rich hues drive up the overall value of Fancy Colored diamonds. We'll discuss these precious beauties later in the chapter.

The D-Z Color Guide

The less color a diamond has, the more valuable it is. The absence of hue is due to the high carbon content of the rock. A colored diamond naturally has less Brilliance and Fire due to the presence of contaminants such as boron and nitrogen. These contaminants not only affect how the carbon atoms are arranged within the diamond, but also absorb and reflect light differently from carbon atoms, resulting in the reflection of different portions of the spectra. This gives the diamond a yellow tinge.

Every color in a ray of light has a different wavelength. When light hits a surface, the atoms in the surface can absorb and reflect some of the wavelengths in the beam of light.

If all the wavelengths in a beam are reflected, the surface appears white. However, if all the wavelengths are absorbed, the surface appears black. Red paint gets its distinct color because the paint pigments absorb all the wavelengths in a beam of light but reflect the wavelength that corresponds to red.

GIA developed five color grades into which diamonds are categorized:

D-F - Colorless. Highest price and quality. Very rare.

G-J - Near colorless.

K-L - Faint yellow.

N-R - Very light yellow.

S-Z - Light yellow.

Creating Optical Illusions

Ideally, you should aim for diamonds that have a Color grade of D-J, but if your pocket dictates that you do otherwise, knowing a few little tricks can help you to create the illusion of an absolutely colorless diamond.

Mother Nature has blessed us with a fundamental flaw. Compared to most other species on the planet, humans have very poor eyesight. It's hard for the naked eye to detect subtle colors and, as such, our eyes and brains can be easily bamboozled.

Some cuts enhance a gem's color. If you've chosen a stone with a lower color grade, avoid cuts like Radiant, Princess and Cushion as these tend to emphasize the unwanted color of your diamond.

The pointed edges of these cuts focuses the light entering the diamond at specific points, thereby giving your stone a more intense hue. Cuts that maximize Brilliance and Fire, such as the Round cut, will help to hide undesired tinges in your gem.

The right setting can be just as important as choosing the cut of your diamond. While the setting may not affect the overall value of your gem, it can bring out all the wonderful nuances and attributes of your diamond, while hiding any undesirables that may be lurking.

Let's say that your new diamond has a tinge of yellow. Choosing a yellow gold setting can combat this dilemma. It sounds strange, but bear with me for a moment.

The whole point is to create an optical illusion. Our brains figure out the true intensity of a color by comparing it against the background. If you place a white T-shirt in a pile of white T-shirts, then its color seems so plain. To your brain, it's just a sea of white

T-shirts so the brilliance of any one shirt doesn't stand out as much.

However, if you take that same shirt and place it next to a darker background, say a dingier shirt or a light cream background, the color of the shirt seems to really pop.

If you've been bitten by the science bug and wish to extend the experiment, then place the shirt against progressively darker backgrounds. The darker the background gets, the whiter the T-shirt appears to be. The shirt hasn't gotten whiter. It's just that our brains now have a better contrast between the object and the background and is therefore better able to distinguish between the colors.

The same principle is at work when choosing a setting. By placing a faint yellow diamond in a yellow gold setting, the contrast between the colors isn't very noticeable. Your brain can't really make out just how yellow your diamond really is.

Of course this rule only works to some extent; trying to make a Z color grade diamond appear as colorless as a D grade stone can't be done with all the magic tricks in the world.

This same optical illusion is also at play in jewelry stores. The lighting in the display case isn't there just for ambience; it is specially chosen to bring out the best qualities of a stone and to make the gems appear closer to colorless than they really are. If you're not sure about the color grade of your desired rock, just ask for the stone's Certificate. Remember the experts are far better at judging a diamond's color than you are.

Feeling confident in your diamond buying skills? Then inspect the stones yourself in normal office light or in sunlight from a window using a Master Chart to make your comparisons. The Master Chart is a standardized color wheel that every reputable jewel dealer should possess. It allows you to compare the color of your gem with that of the standardized color ranges for GIA, or whichever certifying body that has issued the chart.

Fancy Colored Diamonds

Sometimes a girl just has to have a splash of color. If this is the case, then colored diamonds are for you. These stones, often called Fancies, naturally have less Sparkle, Brilliance and Fire because these properties are inhibited by the gem's color.

Most diamonds mined from the depths are colorless or slightly yellow. However, intensely colored natural Fancies are the rarest stones, especially red or green colored Fancies. The color is due to various minerals and elements which got trapped during the formation of the gem. This is the only time in diamond buying history when you *want* to sacrifice Brilliance and Fire for color.

Colored diamonds generally have the largest price tags and, as such, many people opt for cheaper, synthetic Fancies. If you're interested in a ring that has more flash without the price tag, then these stones are a great buy.

Fancies come in every color of the rainbow. Yellow diamonds are the most common, while the rarest hues are red and purple. Other notable colors include pink, blue, gray, black and olive.

A secondary benefit of a Fancy's color is that it hides flaws much better than a regular diamond. Despite this, it is always best to buy a stone with minimal flaws; after all, what good is a vibrantly colored gem if it has Mount Rushmore-sized craters in it.

Also of great importance when it comes to buying Fancies is the gem's Carat Weight. Large, intensely colored natural stones can be fetched for astronomically high prices as they are almost impossible to find. Diamond cutters are all too aware of this and try to maximize the carat weight of a Fancy by choosing cuts and shapes that enhance the gem's color.

Popular diamond shapes for Fancy Colored diamonds are Radiant, Princess and Cushion, since the corners of these shapes encourage light refraction, giving the illusion of a richer, deeper hue.

It is extremely rare to find a Fancy that has an 'Ideal' cut grade since this cut is designed to maximize Brilliance and Fire, two properties that are of lower priority when it comes to Fancy Colored diamonds.

Jewelry manufacturers are also mindful of the setting they choose for Fancies. Yellow Fancy diamonds are usually mounted on white gold or platinum settings in order to highlight the nuances of the diamond's color. This is the same principle that we learned earlier. Sounds confusing? It's about tricking the brain.

The color of the gem appears more vibrant and alive when your brain compares it to the white gold setting. In this case you *want* the color of the diamond to stand out; you want the contrast between the two colors to be drastic, so that nuances of the stone's color are obvious. On the other hand, regular diamonds are supposed to be almost colorless; therefore, a gem with a slight yellow color is best displayed against a yellow gold background in order to hide the stone's color.

Color Treatments

Sometimes diamonds are subjected to a few embellishments in order to make their color more appealing. These treatments are designed solely to increase the gem's resale value. As a budding diamond connoisseur, you should be aware of these little tricks:

Jewelers may apply a non-permanent coating before presenting a diamond to a client.

Natural Fancies are extremely rare and expensive. Diamond manufactures may opt to create synthetic Fancies. Treated gems have significantly reduced value, so it is imperative to find out if your diamond has had any embellishments or treatments.

The sneakiest of jewelers will paint blue or purple dots at the bottom of a Fancy before setting it. When light from within the diamond hits this highly refractive paint, it makes the gem's color seem more vibrant. This is why I encourage you to buy loose diamonds, so that you know exactly what you are paying for.

Fluorescence

Fluorescence is a measure of the intensity of a diamond's glow under an UV light. (black light.) A great analogy is walking under the UV light at a local bar or nightclub. The black lights in the room make a white T-shirt glow; this is Fluorescence.

Due to its chemical and mineral composition, all diamonds glow to some extent. Fluorescence is most prevalent when the rock has traces of boron and nitrogen. Near colorless diamonds have an exceptionally high carbon content and, as such, they won't light up like a nuclear experiment gone awry.

There is still some confusion as to the real significance of Fluorescence on the value of diamond; in some cases it's a good thing. If we assume that all other properties of the diamonds under investigation, i.e. Cut and Clarity, remain the same, a rock with a low color grading can appear almost colorless in normal lighting conditions, if it's highly fluorescent.

However, the reverse is true for diamonds with a high color grade. A high degree of Fluorescence makes gems with D-F color grades look cloudy under normal lighting conditions. In this case, Fluorescence is considered to be a disadvantage; therefore these diamonds will be less expensive.

Whether or not Fluorescence greatly affects the color quality of Fancies is still up in the air. Some schools of thought believe that there's no real impact. A GIA study in 1997 reported that to the naked eye, the presence of Fluorescence in a diamond makes no difference, regardless of the color grade. In this case, our eyes see what we want them to see.

Since Fluorescence tends to whiten colored diamonds, it is probably best to go for Fancies that have as little Fluorescence as possible, just to be on the safe side. Generally speaking, Fluorescence has the least impact of a diamond's value, so don't worry too much if you have a great rock that has a Medium Fluorescence grade.

Chapter 8 – Clarity

Long ago, carbon atoms started to bump into each other and clump together. In the fracas, a few other elements and bits of rock debris got stuck in the middle, and just like a mosquito trapped in some prehistoric amber resin, there was no escape. Even Houdini couldn't pull that one off.

Fast forward a few million years and you have diamonds with all sorts of flaws. As a future diamond buying expert, you must be armed with the knowledge of how these 'wayward extras' can affect the value of your new gem.

As Clear as a Diamond

Diamonds with no wayward extras are tricky to find, but that doesn't mean that they don't exist. It only takes tons of mined rock, sharp eyes and patience to keep you from jumping off a cliff. Kudos to professional diamond sorters and cutters! I mean, who wouldn't snap after seeing the millionth diamond rough that is full of, for lack of a better term, crud? This explains why you'll have a better chance of riding a unicorn through Central Park than finding an absolutely flawless diamond.

All the things that mar these precious beauties can be broken down into two main categories, *Inclusions* and *Blemishes*.

A diamond's impurities and imperfections can be any number of things, from cracks in the diamond to atoms of other elements of the periodic table. These impurities and imperfections are classified according to their location.

Inclusions are the impurities found *within* the diamond, while **Blemishes** are the imperfections (scratches or bumps) located *on* the diamond.

(a) Inclusions

These are categorized according to the appearance of the flaws.

Crystals

During formation, sometimes tiny diamonds get trapped inside larger ones. Crystals can disrupt the reflection of light within your gem, reducing its overall Brilliance.

Pinpoints

Sometimes tiny white spots that resemble a cloud or a cluster can appear within your gem. These are usually impossible to see with the naked eye and aren't usually mentioned in a diamond's Plot unless there's a large group of clouds packed together in a small area of your diamond.

Dark or Black Spots

When tiny carbon deposits get trapped within a diamond, they create black spots. These can sometimes be removed via Laser Drilling which will be discussed in upcoming sections of this chapter.

Cleavage

These are small cracks that are parallel to the normal planes of a diamond. To get an idea of what a diamond cleavage looks like, imagine your windshield being cracked by tiny stones. Cleavages usually occur when the diamond has been struck at an angle that causes it to split.

Feather

This type of inclusion has nothing to do with bird feathers. It's another variation of a crack/cleavage that resembles a feather.

Bearding or Girdle Fringes

Every now and then, even the most experienced diamond cutter has a bad day. When the bruting process doesn't go quite as planned, a cut diamond sometimes develops a 'beard.' Diamond beards result from uneven pressure of the diamond saw and usually appear as dig marks on the girdle.

Growth or Grain Lines

It is not uncommon for diamonds to have variations in the hardness of their surface. When the gem is polished, these variations can lead to grain lines. Grain lines are mostly visible when a diamond is rotated too slowly during polishing. Once present, grain lines are nearly impossible to remove without cutting away the diamond.

Knaat or Twin Lines

Imagine something that looks like a comet trail within your diamond. These extend to the surface of your gem and are a sign of a diamond that's structurally compromised. If the gem that you are interested in has a Knaat (sometimes called a Knot), it's best to avoid buying this stone. The stresses of daily wear and tear will cause your new gem to shatter like a block of melting ice being hit by a sledgehammer.

Drill Channels

When a diamond is laser drilled, the drill channels created can be visible after the fact. This is one telltale sign that your gem's clarity has been enhanced.

Needles

These are long thin crystals that sometimes give the diamond a more interesting look.

Intergrowths

When multiple types of flaws occur in one spot, the resultant imperfection is referred to as an Intergrowth. Usually Intergrowths are a mixture of needles, pinpoints and feathers, but any other combination of Inclusions can be classified as an Intergrowth.

(b) Blemishes

Blemishes are surface imperfections that are usually caused by wear and tear or occur during setting.

Naturals

Sometimes unpolished areas of the outer surface of a rough diamond are still visible in the finished stone. This occurs when the cutter is trying to make the largest possible cut diamond from the rough stone and has simply run out of enough material to finish cutting the diamond. Naturals are a sign of a good cutter because it means there is minimum wastage of a rough rock. These unfinished parts are usually on the girdle and don't affect the stones performance.

Nicks and Scratches

The daily wear and tear of a busy life can lead to little cuts on your diamond. Nicks are prevalent on a diamond's Girdle since this part isn't usually protected by the setting. Scratches are simply long nicks. A bit of re-polishing will make your gem as good as new.

Polish Lines

When a jeweler does not properly maintain his equipment, lines can develop while polishing your diamond. Re-polishing with a new polishing wheels will solve this dilemma.

Girdle Roughness

This blemish appears as crisscrossed lines on the girdle and can be removed by re-polishing.

Pits or Cavities

Microscopic holes on the diamond's Table are called Pits. These can greatly reduce a diamond's Clarity, even though they're impossible to spot with the naked eye. Larger holes are called cavities and usually occur when a diamond cutter removes an inclusion near the surface of the stone.

Fractures

These are large gouges that run along the plane of a diamond's facet. The process of enhancing a diamond's Clarity, known as Fracture Filling, was initially invented to correct this type of imperfection.

Chips

When diamonds are victims of rough handling, tiny bits can break off. This is mostly seen in the culet since it's generally the most fragile point on a diamond. There are two simple solutions to this issue: have your diamond undergo enhancement treatments and, most importantly, be gentle with your gem.

Many people mistakenly think of inclusions and blemishes as being all bad. Just like our freckles, moles and laugh lines, these imperfections give a diamond some character and spunk, making your gem truly unlike any other. Diamonds are like fingerprints; no two will ever be exactly alike.

(c) Under the Jeweler's Loupe

Diamonds are best viewed under a microscope, but in the absence of one, a jeweler's loupe works well too. Have you ever seen those old spy films where the villain uses a small glass to inspect the latest shipment of diamonds? That's a jeweler's loupe. Any jeweler worth his salt will have one.

Note that I've said a jeweler's loupe, not a magnifying glass. Under no circumstances should you accept a magnifying glass since this does not give the appropriate magnification. If you wanted to relive your high school biology days, you would have asked for one. You're there to buy diamonds, not dissect frogs!

Using a loupe can be a bit tricky. Firstly you must hold the loupe with the hand that is on the side of the eye that you'll be using. So if you're using your left eye to look through the loupe, then use your right hand to hold the instrument. Using the opposite hand can lead to wobbling and you might not get a crystal clear view of the gem. Easy does it; you want to have the steady hands of a surgeon.

It may sound counter-intuitive, but keep both eyes open when looking through the loupe. The tendency is to close one eye, but doing so puts more strain on the eye that is open. A diamond plot is a good general guide to use while examining your gem. It's a map of your diamond, indicating where inclusions and blemishes are located.

But most importantly, take your time. Flaws can be hard to spot, so never rush through this process.

If, however, you can't be bothered with all that, you can always rely on the certificate of your gem from a reputable source. The professionals will be much better at spotting the flaws than you will ever be, though it doesn't hurt to have a little extra knowledge.

Always inspect loose diamonds to ensure you're really getting the Clarity Grade that you're paying for. Sometimes the color of the setting or the position of the setting's prongs can obscure flaws. If this is absolutely impossible, it's ok to buy mounted stones, but, as always, insist on certificates.

Diamond Clarity Grades

Remember that the creation of diamonds in Nature requires extreme conditions; therefore it isn't uncommon for things to go awry. Sometimes little bubbles, warps or other imperfections are caused by the presence of stray elements or cracks and these flaws can't be removed during cutting. Diamonds are categorized according to the level of imperfections they contain. The larger the size and number of flaws that a diamond has, the lower its clarity grade will be and, ultimately, the cheaper its price.

Cut gems are inspected and viewed at 10x magnification under a microscope or via a jeweler's loupe, and are sorted accordingly. The sorted diamonds are categorized into one of six clarity grades:

Flawless (FL)

Perfection at its finest. These gems have no bumps, scratches, blemishes, black spots, or feathers; absolutely no flaws at all. However, perfection is a rare treat just like a shot of the world's most expensive, the 64 year old Macallan, while on your unicorn ride. Flawless diamonds are almost impossible to find. Almost.

Internally Flawless (IF)

As the name implies, these beauties have no inclusions and only minuscule blemishes on the surface. If you desire the absolute best, this is the closest thing to a perfect diamond available on the market. Unlike lower grade levels, this category is not sub-divided; a diamond is either Internally Flawless or not.

Very, Very Small Inclusions (VVS)

For the very picky among us, VVS diamonds are just right. The flaws are only visible as tiny pinpoints in very small amounts, when viewed under a microscope. A jeweler's loupe will not help you at all.

Very Small Inclusions (VS)

You'll find a bit more imperfections in these than you would in any of the previous grade levels, but they're still not visible to the naked eye. This group is further sub-divided into two categories: VS1 and VS2. VS diamonds are a good buy if you are a bit fussy about the visibility of imperfections and are willing to dole out the cash to avoid them. Anything below this level will not fit your tastes.

Small Inclusions (SI)

Imperfections in SI diamonds are obvious under a microscope but are still invisible to the naked eye. The visibility of inclusions can be 'Easy' (SI1), 'Very Easy' (SI2), and 'Almost Obvious.' (SI3.) Unless your friends and family are walking around with their own loupes or have bionic eyes, they won't be able to see the flaws. SI diamonds are a great bargain if you're watching the household budget.

Included (I)

The visibility of imperfections is sub-divided into three categories: 'Easy' (I1), 'Very Easy' (I2) and 'Obvious' (I3) under 10x magnification. The inclusions and blemishes of diamonds in this grade level are as obvious as missing teeth in a sparkling smile. As such

'Imperfect' diamonds are dirt cheap; most are usually subjected to enhancement treatments in order to improve their resale value.

If you're blown away by a great deal being offered on a rock you absolutely love, check again, it's probably an enhanced diamond.

Inspect your gem from every angle, not just from the table. Sometimes inclusions that are invisible from the diamond's Table are noticeable from its Pavilion. Just keep in mind that diamonds are graded from the table.

Clarity Enhanced Diamonds

An experienced diamond cutter will choose a shape, cut and setting that will hide any flaws the stone has. For those that still come through, jewelers turn to various enhancement treatments that will make a gem appear flawless. It's all about playing up the Illusion.

If a flawless diamond is a smidge out of your reach, then try getting clarity enhanced gems. These are diamonds that have been treated to make their blemishes and inclusions less visible to the naked eye. Clarity Enhanced diamonds are a great way to get good quality rocks without a humongous price tag. Enhancing a gem's clarity does not affect its overall value or quality. It simply makes it easier for jewelers to sell diamonds that have a few inclusions in them.

Diamond houses use two main techniques to enhance the clarity of their diamonds, Fracture Filling and Laser Drilling. Each technique is used to cover up a particular type of flaw, and each has particular advantages and disadvantages.

If a deal on a breathtaking gem seems too good to be true, it usually is. Always find out whether or not a diamond has been enhanced before you purchase. Clarity Enhanced diamonds run cheaper than almost flawless rocks, although both are indistinguishable to the naked eye. It's best to ask to view the gem under magnification (using a jeweler's loupe) or get the gem's certificate as there are shady sellers who'll try to pass off an enhanced diamond at the price of an almost flawless gem.

Don't be duped! You don't want to pay more for a rock than it's really worth.

(a) Fracture Filling

In 1982, an Israeli scientist named Zvi Yehuda invented a process for making flawed diamonds appear perfect. By treating a diamond with a highly refractive liquid-like silicon oil under high pressure and temperature, he was able to fill some of the cracks in the diamond. His procedure is now commonplace in today's diamond industry. Fracture Filled diamonds are the cheapest of all Clarity Enhanced diamonds.

This technique is a great fix for those pesky feathers in your diamond, but Fracture filled diamonds tend to be more fragile than their Laser Drilled cousins. They become dislodged when the gem is placed in boiling acids, ammonia or under excessive heat and pressure. The fillings tend to fall out during setting when extreme heat and pressure are used to mount a gem onto its metal pedestal. A skilled jeweler should be able to overcome that issue; after all, you're only going to buy the rock, not mount it!

If, however, you happen to dip your hand in ammonia or boiling acid, then a blemished diamond is the least of your concerns.

Fracture filled diamonds display certain telltale signs. When viewed under magnification, these diamonds tend to throw flashes of color which are not typically seen when the gems are rotated. The presence of a few trapped air bubbles is also another hint that your rock has been Fracture filled.

Since Fracture filled diamonds are less durable, government regulations dictate that a jeweler must disclose whether or not a gem has been Fracture filled *before* it's purchased. Your jeweler should offer a warranty to repair the diamond if its filling ever comes loose.

(b) Laser Drilling

"Out, damned spot! Out, I say."

(William Shakespeare. *Macbeth*, Act 5, Scene 1, line 39.)

Sometimes nothing gets rid of a spot like a high powered laser beam. Laser drilling bores minuscule holes within a diamond in an effort to correct black spots and other types of Inclusions. These inclusions are usually carbon deposits.

Once the laser reaches the carbon spot, the diamond is dipped in acid which will eat away the deposit.

Since this type of treatment is permanent, there's no fear of the inclusion reappearing as with fracture filled diamonds.

Laser drilled diamond generally run cheaper than almost flawless diamonds, but pricier than their fracture filled counterpart. However, laser drilling renders a gem somewhat fragile, so doing excessively brutal physical activities while wearing your laser drilled rock may not be the wisest thing.

Unlike their fracture filled friends, laser treated diamonds will survive professional cleaning and heat exposure and, since drill channels are narrower than a strand of hair, dirt and debris have a tough time getting into these holes.

It isn't uncommon for a diamond to undergo both enhancement techniques. The gem is first drilled and then the channels are filled with a clear, highly refractive liquid (usually silicone oil). In this case, the fix is not permanent, as the filling may come loose and the jeweler must report this enhancement before you purchase the stone.

Avoid diamonds that have been laser drilled too often. If your new gem has more holes than a slice of Swiss cheese, it's a sign that the original diamond is of relatively poor quality. Laser drilling weakens the gem's integrity, albeit by a small fraction. 'Swiss Cheese gems will be noticeably weaker and can shatter easily.

To Enhance or Not to Enhance?

The answer to that depends on what you're most comfortable with. If you're a purist who goes to great lengths to ensure that your Louis Vuitton bag is actually from Louis Vuitton, then clarity enhanced diamonds may not be your cup of tea.

If you choose the Clarity Enhanced route, then laser drilled beauties are your best bet. They may be pricier than their fracture filled cousins, but you'll rest easier knowing that the fix is permanent.

Since the gem is valued in its original form, Enhancement will not affect its value. If a gem with a few inclusions is worth $1000 before it's enhanced, it will still be worth $1000 afterwards. The only difference is that now you can't see the inclusions anymore. Enhanced gems run cheaper not because they've been enhanced, but because the original gem had visible flaws that diminished its value. Enhancement only makes a flawed gem more sellable. The only people who will know that your jewel was enhanced will be you and the jeweler, so your secret is safe.

However, if you're a purist through and through, then you'll have that nagging feeling in the back of your head every time you look at your enhanced diamond. To ease your suffering, you may need to cough up the extra cash for an almost flawless diamond; after all, perfection comes at a price.

My only advice in this matter is that your jeweler must be upfront about any enhancements *before* you buy the diamond. This is why it is so important to get certified gems; you'll know exactly what you're paying for.

Chapter 9 – Carats, not Carrots!

Gentlemen, she may not say it, but your Fair Maiden expects you to slip an exquisite diamond ring on her trembling hand when you pop The Question. You can thank The De Beers Diamond Company for that! In 1939 they published the first diamond engagement ring ad campaign to persuade men to buy these pricey little gems for the future Mrs., and just like that, the old 'Ball n' Chain' was diamond encrusted.

Nowadays, more couples are opting for alternative gems, but the vast majority of engagement rings on the market are still diamond mounted. It is now the symbol of Love; Cupid is flying around throwing diamonds at couples instead of arrows.

In the Court of Public Opinion, the size of the diamond in the engagement ring is directly proportional to how much your Knight-In-Shining-Armor (or your Fair Maiden) loves you. Don't believe me? Take a look at the ever increasing size of celebrity engagement rings.

Ahh, Carats!

Those wonderful little numbers are as important to a diamond as body measurements are to a supermodel. But what exactly are carats, how are they measured and how do they affect buying diamonds?

Carats, not to be confused with karats (gold) or carrots, (Bugs Bunny's favorite dish) are a measure of the mass of a diamond. Simply put, it's the weight of your 'Bling.' One Carat is equivalent to 200 milligrams.

However, simply stating a diamond's Carat Weight does not really give a true reflection of its size, just as hearing someone's weight does not really tell you whether or not that person has a healthy Body Mass Index (BMI). You must also take into account his height.

A 5'10" person that weighs 150 lbs looks very different from someone of the same weight who's 4'8" tall. You have to use more than one point of comparison in order to get a truer image of the size and ultimately of the value of an object. When it comes to a diamond's Carat Weight, there are also two very important factors to consider, the distance across its top and the rock's Cut grade.

What's The View From Above?

Does the diamond look symmetrical and elegant, or squatty and clunky, especially when placed on your fingers (or next to the body part on which the diamond will be worn)? Even a million dollar gem with a massive carat weight can look like a Cracker Jack box toy if it's disproportionate to your fingers.

You want people to stop and say 'WOW!' and admire the whole ensemble, both you and the ring. If they forget that you're attached to it, then you've got the wrong size gem for your features. Not everybody can pull off a huge rock with style.

How Carats affect your wallet

The term *Carat* is derived from the Greek word κεράτιον, meaning 'fruit of the Carob.' Carob seeds were used by ancient traders as a counterweight when measuring precious metals and stones. In the Roman Empire, one pure gold coin was equal in weight to 24 Carob seeds.

A diamond's Carat Weight has a huge impact on its price, even if the diamond is of a lower cut quality. The tiniest increase in the size of the diamond results in the disproportionately large leap in its price. Large carat gems are typically in higher demand and much harder to find. Remember the good old economic principle of Supply and Demand?

Splurge on your wedding or honeymoon by saving money on your rings. Diamonds that do not have half or full carat weights are always significantly cheaper. A 0.95 carat diamond will be cheaper than a 1.00 carat gem but, to the naked eye, there's no difference in the actual size of the rock.

The 'Carat Conundrum'

As with all things, size comes at a price. Don't be fooled into thinking that a big ring automatically means better quality. Large carat diamonds are a lot like cute jocks in 1980s high school movies; big but not very brilliant.

This 'Carat Conundrum' arises from the fact that bigger stones must be cut outside of the calculated proportions for maximum Brilliance. As stated earlier, diamonds are cut according to the dimensions using Tolkowsky's formulae. If the diamond is cut larger than these proportions, then various facets within the stone will not be angled for maximum reflection, ergo, not as much light bounces around within the diamond.

If there's one thing we've already learned, when it comes to diamonds, it's the shine that counts most. And you thought high school geometry was useless!

A diamond's Cut grade is always of great significance even when choosing the size of your gem. It is always better to have a rock with a smaller Carat Weight but a higher Cut grade than vice-versa.

What about you? What are your needs and desires as it relates to your diamond ring? If your Love desires a ring so large that he/she needs to hire a few assistants from Craigslist to help carry the thing around, then by all means, go for it!

However, sometimes 'Creating the Illusion' works just as wonderfully without the need to sell a kidney. Mounting several smaller stones in a pattern can look aesthetically more pleasing than placing a single large stone in the setting. In this case, the Total Carat Weight (TCW) would be factored into the purchase price and, depending on your choice of stones, can run cheaper than buying one large, bulky gem. Choosing long diamond shapes, like the Marquise, or a high-pronged setting will add oomph to a tiny rock without making your wallet limp and lifeless.

Also consider the physical proportions of the wearer. If your Maiden or Knight has very slender features, a smaller carat diamond will appear proportionately much larger than it really is. As such, packing a larger carat on her tiny finger is comparable to forcing Mount Everest onto a twig; the beauty of the entire ensemble is lost by the very thing that's supposed to enhance.

Chapter 10 – Cost

Money is an integral part of the Laws of Nature, second only to Gravity. Some lucky devils never seem to have any wallet issues at all, but for those of us on a Soda Budget, our first thought is usually 'Can I afford it?'

When you only have enough for a 1998 hatchback, getting that 2011 Bugatti Veyron 16.4 Super Sport may be a few gigantic leaps out of your reach. Knowing your price range can help you decide on the type of car to purchase. Being a savvy diamond connoisseur can score you fantastic deals on the ring of her dreams.

Your Total Will Be...

Buying a diamond is confusing enough without stressing over the cost. Have you ever heard of The *Rappaport Price List* or 'Rap List?' It's a monthly guide to the wholesale market prices of diamonds. This list is often used by diamond dealers and wholesalers to calculate the price of their wares according to current market conditions. It provides a good starting point, but bear in mind that because so many factors are used to estimate the cost of a diamond, the list can get confusing to use and your estimated price may be off by thousands. Prices can also vary wildly depending on the mark-up of the retailer.

If you're unsure about using this list, then leave it to the professionals who have years of experience figuring out its intricacies.

(a) Reading the Rap List

For the more adventurous amongst us, here's a quick guide to reading your Rap List. Bear in mind that the figure you'll get from the list is only a base price; it does not take into account several other key factors such as a diamond's cut, the presence of Fluorescence, a gem's polish and its measurements, all of which can raise or lower the price calculated using the list. Also don't forget the merchant's mark up!

For copyright reasons, I cannot actually include a copy of the Rappaport List in this book, but let's work in the realm of the hypothetical. If you have managed to score a Rap List from a very friendly dealer, thank him whole-heartedly and get ready to do a little price hunting of your own.

Let's say you want a 2.30 carat Round, you would locate the section in your Rap List that deals with the Cut and Carat Weight that you're interested in.

Note that these are arbitrary numbers and not those actually reflected in the Rappaport List. I've used these numbers just to give you a general idea of how to use the Rap List.

Rappaport List Sample

Round Cuts (2.00 - 2.99 CT) 28/06/12

Clarity Grade

Color Grade	IF	VVS1	**VVS2**	VS1	VS2	S1	S2	I1
D		200	190	170	80	60	50	30 20
E		180	169	164	77	59	47	28 19
F		175	152	140	67	49	41	26 17

Now that you have located the section that deals with the cut and carat that you want, we can proceed with estimating the price of your dream gem. First, choose your desired color grade from the left hand side of the list. In this case, you want nothing but the best for your 'Sweetie', so let's say that your hypothetical ring will have a 'D' color grade.

Now, what Clarity grade are you looking for? Do you want an Internally Flawless diamond, or will an 'eye-clean' gem do just fine? Let's say that you want a VVS2 diamond for your ring; well just scroll across to the VVS2 column. The number that you find there is then multiplied by 100 in order to get your carat price. The result of that calculation is then multiplied by the carat weight of your gem to get the base price for your desired diamond.

So the cost of our Round cut diamond with a 'D' color grade and VVS2 clarity will be calculated like this:

190 (from our sample table) x 100 = $19,000

Since our actual carat weight is 2.30, then the calculated cost of our desired diamond is: $19,000 x 2.30 = $43,700.

Seems simple, so why all the hype about how confusing it is? Well, this price does not include other features of the diamond that can drive its value up or down. If your diamond has a Fluorescence grade of 'Faint' then there's no change in the estimated price, but Polish and Symmetry grades of 'Very Good' tack on about 2% a piece. Now a total of 4% has been added to your base price of $39,100. You can factor in an additional 10% if your diamond has a cut grade of 'Very Good' and, since our gem is certified, you can increase the estimated price by another 2%.

Let's not forget about the retailer's mark-up! Exceptional customer service and advice, lifetime warranties and additional services like the setting can run at least an extra 20%. So, all in all, you have added 36% to your base price; your lovely gem will now squeeze $53,176 from your pocket.

Of course you know this figure is not an exact price. Please don't get upset if your retailer doesn't have this sample rock for $53,176. The numbers and percentages stated here are just for illustrative purposes. The actual price tag for your gem will vary depending on many different factors. The aim here is to understand how to use the Rap List, not to give actual price quotations.

Generally, it is a safe bet to tack on an additional **40%** on any estimated price; it sounds like a lot, but it's better to overestimate the price of your diamond. That way, if the rock of your dreams turns out to be cheaper in reality, you can always splurge on a diamond upgrade or for lavish bubble baths in champagne on your honeymoon

(b) Saving Towards Your Dream Diamond

So you've decide to take the leap and surprise your Love with a ring. However, that growing collection of pocket dust bunnies and bottle caps is not going to get the rock of her dreams. Your bride to be deserves so much more than a carnival popcorn ring, but you can't buy Beluga Caviar when you're working with a Soda Budget. What do you do?

First of all, don't feel overwhelmed. Remember that information is your greatest asset when navigating the confusing world of buying jewelry and, believe me, you have garnered quite a bit so far. You have an idea of what to get. Now let's start funding the dream.

The most important thing to do is to establish a budget and be prepared to adjust your diamond wish list to meet that budget. That means facing the cold, harsh truth of your financial reality. Before shopping around, it's best to have an idea of how much you can afford, how you intend to finance your purchase and the repayment plan. It's easier to adjust your rock to your budget, than to adjust your budget to your rock.

There's more to the ring than the sales price. When you factor in the cost of insurance, major repairs like resizing, and independent appraisals, just to name a few, the cost of your diamond ring can become sky high. The shock of your diamond's price tag can leave you feeling like you've just been slapped in the face.

When saving towards your ring, it's wise to keep the money separate from your regular savings and expense accounts. Stash it in a separate account, under the mattress, in an old shoe box, wherever. Just don't touch that money! Pretend it doesn't even exist until you're ready to buy your rock.

Cutting back on unnecessary expenses can help you score some extra cash. Do you really need that extra latte in the mornings? Is your membership fee really that important if you never go to the gym? This is all just a temporary sacrifice and after the big day, you can go back to your 'pre-penny pinching' ways.

Sometimes, saving means cutting back on the diamond itself. Taking a gem with flaws that aren't obvious, i.e. a stone that is 'eye-clean' can save you a fortune. It is doubtful that any relatives will walk around with a jeweler's loupe and do daily inspections of your diamond since you're not in a diamond boot-camp. What really matters is the love of your significant other, not the hunt for the 'impossibly perfect' ring.

Online or In-Store

On the path to becoming a diamond connoisseur, you need to familiarize yourself with the options available for buying your rock. Should you stalk your diamond prey online or trek down to your local Mom & Pop jewelry store? Either way, the value of the stone doesn't change; a diamond valued at $1000 will always be valued at $1000, whether online or in-store. The difference in price arises from the perks and mark-up that accompanies the gem.

In general, online prices are slightly cheaper than retail, but there is a reason for this difference. In a jewelry store, you're paying for one-on-one advice, a chance to examine the gem up close and personal, the ability to negotiate prices to a more comfortable level, and to pick up a few extra perks that would not otherwise be easily accessible online.

In-store jewelry can sometimes carry a massive mark-up, so it is always savvy to be on the lookout for anything that can drive the price down a bit. Don't be shy to ask for discounts on the retail price or for additional perks in your after sales package. In the worst case scenario, your jeweler will say 'No,' or at best, he'll give you a discount. Push the limit and ask for a discount to see how far your jeweler is willing to go.

It is impossible to overemphasize the importance of buying gems from reputable dealers. You are less likely to be bamboozled, get higher quality stones and better after sales service from a reputable, licensed dealer, whether online or at a Brick & Mortar store. Would you buy a ring from a street side chicken shack? I don't think so!

There's no way to say which method is better; it all rests on your comfort level, what you are willing to pay for, and what you expect from your diamond buying experience. If you angrily throw your phone into the TV whenever you call your local service provider and get the automated customer support line, then a face-to-face with a good jeweler is more your style. If not, then an online retailer might work for you.

Chapter 11 – Confidence & Certificates - Prove It!

Say it with me now, Certificates are your friends.

Would you buy a used car without a Vehicle History Report? After all, you cannot be certain that sweet, blue-haired grandma from whom you are buying your car hasn't been doing some illegal street racing with her peeps at nights. So why buy a diamond without certification? Credentials must always be verified and diamonds are no exception to this rule. But what does one look for in a certified diamond? How does John Q. Public make heads or tails of diamond certificates?

What Are Certified Diamonds?

In a nutshell, they're diamonds with credentials; a Diamond History Report. These credentials are often given after a diamond has undergone extensive testing by highly reputable gemological labs. The gemologists at these certifying bodies are experts who live, eat and breathe diamonds; they are highly capable at objectively examining and discerning all the nuances of each gemstone.

Why are Certificates so important?

The short answer is for authenticity and security.

Certified diamonds command better prices simply because their authenticity can be proven. When a gem's characteristics have been verified by reputable professionals, potential buyers feel much more confident that they are not being swindled into buying a sub-par diamond. However, it's important to know what to look for in a DQR and to bear in mind that fakes and scammers are everywhere. So watch out!

A certificate also helps to prevent theft when the gem is brought in for professional cleaning or repairs. Dishonest jewelers and repair personnel are less likely to make a switch for an inferior stone because your gem has all the necessary paperwork and is therefore easily recognizable.

Reputable labs are independent of the various points of sale of diamond and, as such, they have no share of the take from dishonest diamond retailers. These labs will more objectively judge a diamond than small, start up labs which are often connected to diamond dealers. Crooked gemologists from these start-up labs will of course give your gem a grade that benefits themselves and their partners in order to share in the profits. Sneaky, sneaky!

(a) Gemological Institute of America (GIA)

A world leader in gemology, GIA is a non-profit organization created in 1931 to provide training for gemologist and certification services. It has several locations worldwide including offices in New York, London, Tokyo and Antwerp just to name a few.

Famous stones that have been certified by GIA include *The Hope Diamond*, Elizabeth Taylor's engagement ring (known as *The Taylor-Burton Ring*) and *the Millennium Star* diamond.

GIA is considered the 'Crème de la Crème' and is notorious for having the most exacting guidelines for testing diamonds. As such, sellers will always boast that their diamonds are GIA-certified. The lab offers two types of DQRs, but both contain basically the same information.

Diamond Grading Reports (DGRs)

DGRs are not generated for Synthetic, fracture filled or mounted diamonds and the price of these reports vary depending on the carat weight of diamond being examined. These reports contain all the standard information related to the gem including: the 4Cs, the proportions of the stone in millimeters, the Finish and the diamond's Plot.

Diamond Dossiers (DD)

Diamond Dossiers are usually issued for stones smaller than 1.50 carats. These reports are much cheaper than DGRs and contain the same information excluding the diamond's Plot. Laser inscription services are also included in this service.

The price for laser inscription varies according to the size of the stone being inscribed and the desired length of the inscription number. Larger stones or longer numbers command more cash.

(b) American Gem Society (AGS)

Established in 1996, the AGS lab prides itself on providing accurate reports with quick turnover times. The labs are located worldwide in the popular diamond cities such as Antwerp and work in collaboration with Rappaport laboratories (of the Rap List fame).

AGS offers several types of certificates and reports but the most important one is the Diamond Quality Report. The DQR has most of the same information as the GIA reports but, unlike GIA, AGS scores its gems on a 0 -

10 scale, with 0 being perfect and 10 being the worst.

(c) European Gemological Laboratory (EGL USA)

The EGL was created in 1974 to fulfill the growing need for reliable, accurate diamond certificates. EGLs are located in the diamond processing hubs worldwide, but there is a distinction between EGL USA and EGL International. Although both started from the same parent company, the US based subsidiary has been under private ownership since 1986.

EGL USA offers two main diamond certificates for Natural and Fancy Colored diamonds.

Diamond Certificate

EGL USA certificates contain most of the standard information you've come to expect from diamond certificates such as a diamond's Cut, Color and Clarity grades, Carat weight and Plot.

Colored Diamond Analysis Reports

This report is specifically created for Colored Diamonds. It states the origin of Color (Natural or Synthetic), Color grade, a color photograph of the stone and the standard information such as the stone's Plot, the diamond's proportions and Carat Weight.

(d) Hoge Raad Voor Diamant (HRD)

This non-profit organization is based in Antwerp, Europe's leading diamond city. HRD was established in 1976 to meet the demands for reliable, objective diamond certification in Europe. The Antwerp World Diamond Centre (AWDC) is the main stakeholder in HRD labs.

(e) The Antwerp World Diamond Centre (AWDC) was established in 1973 as a part of HRD, AWDC represents the interests of the Belgian Diamond Industry in the international diamond market.

HRD provides three different types of diamond reports, of which the Diamond Certificate is the most popular and most detailed. The lab also seals its tested diamonds in a package that resembles a credit card. This service ensures that the stone can be safely displayed without incurring scratches, and since the stone is usually sealed with its accompanying certificate, this feature makes it easier to keep track of your diamond's paperwork.

(f) International Gemological Institute (IGI)

Founded in 1975 in Antwerp, IGI labs are located in worldwide diamond processing cities including New York.

IGI provides a series of diamond certificates and colored stone reports. In addition to these reports, IGI offers a diamond seal service similar to that offered by HRD as well as appraising precious heirlooms and priceless diamond pieces without the need to dismantle these delicate pieces.

To avoid being bamboozled by bogus paperwork, it is always wise to check for security features in your report. Each lab has its own combination of features including embossed logos, watermarks and micro lines, to ensure that certificates are not easily forgotten.

PART 2 - WHAT TO EXPECT, WHEN YOU'RE EXPECTING DIAMONDS

By now, you should be well on your way to becoming a diamond aficionado so you can march confidently into your local jewelry store to make a purchase. But before you strut your diamond knowledge to adoring fans, I must warn you that we have only just begun to delve into this subject matter. We've got the basics down, so let's start adding a few layers.

Part 2 of this book deals with the all the issues that arise after you have identified and are in the process of purchasing the diamond of your dreams. Included in this section are many helpful tips on how to look for scams, diamond insurance and how to care for your new gem. If you have hit a brick wall trying to figure out which stone to get for your soon-to-be significant other, I have jotted down a few helpful tips to get you out of that horrible jam.

Now that you've graduated from 'Diamonds 101,' welcome to the advanced classes.

Chapter 12 Avoid the Traps

It's a sad reality, but it's very common for budding diamond connoisseurs to fall prey to either the simplest of errors or the sneakiest of retailers. By not carefully reading the fine print or keeping your wits about you, it's easy to be bamboozled by dealers who are all too happy to assist you in parting with your money.

Diamond Buying Faux Pas

Sometimes, whether due to lack of knowledge or dealing with a stressful situation, we make foolish mistakes that can end up costing thousands. These are unavoidable, but they can be mitigated if you are aware of possible pitfalls.

Being Misled By A Large Carat Weight

Diamonds that are cut too deep rack up carat points without making your gem look bigger. By avoiding these stones, you're ensuring that the extra Carat Weight counts when you buy a large carat diamond. In essence, you are paying extra for something that isn't noticeable.

Purchasing Gems that are Already Set

Jewelers can set diamonds to hide their flaws, making it impossible to accurately judge a diamond's Color and Clarity. The same trick we employed earlier to fool our eyes and brains are now being use to fool you. If your rock costs more than $2000, it is worth the extra hassle of examining it unset or loose. Dealers never buy their wares set; they take every precaution to ensure that they know exactly what they are buying; so should you.

Believing the Hype

Branding and Marketing is designed to grab the consumers' attention and make them instinctively associate a product with a particular action or chore. When you hear the word 'Cookies,' what's the first thing that pops into you head? Your first thought was probably one of the popular brands of cookies like Oreos or Chips Ahoy. Companies invest billions to make sure that happens almost instinctively by using gimmicks like fantastic names or catchy phrases.

Diamond dealers also employ the same techniques. They sometimes give cut stones elaborate names like 'Incredible Cut' or 'Fire Gem' to give you the illusion that you're buying the best stone available. To add to the hype, retailers will place these stones next to noticeably inferior gems. Unsuspecting consumers will see the marked difference in quality and pay top dollar for a gem that's far from fiery. A quick glance of the diamond's certificate will give you an objective perspective without the hype and hoax.

Viewing in Poor Light

The lighting in a typical jewelry store is designed to make its wares sparkle, glimmer and generally look fantastic. Unless you never intend to leave the store, this is of no use to you. It's a good idea to ask to see the gem under normal lighting conditions, like a normal office light or normal sunlight (near a large window). Of course, this is tricky. The jeweler may think that you're about to pull a fast one so it takes some skill to convince him otherwise.

Rounding Up

It's human nature to round a number to the nearest whole number (math classes are coming back to haunt you). Jewelers sometimes round up the carat weight of a stone to the nearest whole number. For example, a 0.90 carat stone can be quoted as a light 1.00 carat gem. The process is technically legal, but unfortunately you're paying for an extra 0.10 carat that's not in your stone. While the figure may seem small, consider that 0.10 carat can cost extra depending on the mark-up and the quality of the diamond.

Make sure that you get the exact Carat Weight and, by extension, the exact price per carat weight. It may sound like nit-picking, but why pay more for something that you're not getting.

Thinking That All Certificates Are Created Equal

It is crucial to know the difference between a GIA certified diamond and a diamond that is certified by a GIA trained gemologist. Sounds weird but there's a difference. A GIA certified diamond has been tested and verified in GIA laboratories under standardized GIA conditions by trained gemologists. The gemologists have no idea where the diamonds originated from. As such, they can more objectively grade the stone. GIA guidelines have built in protocols which maintain a level of anonymity.

On the other hand, a diamond that has been certified by a GIA trained gemologist may not be subject to the same stringent conditions as a GIA certified gem. To gain street credit, a jeweler will often send one of his employees to be trained by GIA. A diamond certified by this individual is not done under the same exacting conditions as it would've been if it were tested at the GIA labs. There is no degree of anonymity, therefore the gem isn't always objectively examined and tested.

Being Surprised by Treatments

A third of all cut diamonds processed have been treated or embellished in some way. These little tweaks may make the diamond look flawless and more appealing to a buyer but they diminish the value of the rock. If you don't mind that your diamond has been enhanced, then by all means go for it. However if you're a child of purity, this may not be for you. This is why reputable certificates are so vital; unless you've got bionic senses, you can't tell on-the-spot that your gem has been treated. A good DQR can give you all that information in a few seconds.

Buying Without A Written Warranty

If you buy diamonds, you're entitled to a warranty of some sort. Most times, you'll get verbal warranty, but if things go south, that holds as much weight in a court of law as a basket holds water. Before you buy, always ask for a written warranty and more importantly, ask to slowly go over it with the jeweler.

Let him explain it to you plainly and in the presence of your own witnesses. I'm not trying to insult your intelligence but sometimes retailers gloss over liability details. They may highlight the items that will attract customers but skip over things that may put them in a bad light. You may hear:

'Free cleanings and repairs for life.'

However, the fine print may read:

'Free cleanings and repairs for life if the gem is brought in by its registered owner on a Tuesday afternoon at 1 pm and is only applicable once every 4 years in the month of March.'

See what I mean?

Not Having Your New Diamond Independently Appraised

Whether for insurance purposes or your own peace of mind, it is vital to have your new gem appraised by an independent, reputable appraiser. It can be done by any of the aforementioned labs, or any other reputable lab in your area. You must first establish the true value of your gem since the sales price is usually the true value of the diamond plus all the retailer's financial embellishments. Asking the appraiser to write a report on your diamond is a neat way to avoid 'The Switcheroo' scam. (See next section.)

An Appraisal and a Certificate are two different things.

An **Appraisal** indicates how much a diamond is worth. I.e. its market value. This is usually derived by using information in the diamond's certificate. Each characteristic of a gem has a particular monetary value.

A **Certificate** only indicates the quality of the diamond, whether it's a polished, Emerald cut with VVS1 clarity and 'D' grade color. Certificates make no mention of the monetary value of the gem.

Hiding Your Laser Inscribed Number

Most certified diamonds have a serial number inscribed in them. This number should match the one on the gem's certificate and be visible when viewed under a microscope or through a loupe. It is important to note the serial number, where it is located on your diamond and ensure that your jeweler doesn't obscure this number during setting. If the number is partially or fully hidden, then it's all too easy for a sneaky jeweler to pull 'The Switcheroo' on you.

Buying Popular Carat Sizes

This may come as a shocker to you, but popular diamond sizes command more moolah than unknown sizes. Any diamond that has a Carat Weight that is a whole number or a half of a whole number usually costs double or triple the price of any other sizes. A 1.00 carat diamond will cost more than a 0.90 gem. It's a smarter move to choose a diamond that's an unpopular size; that way you can get more for your money.

Shopping In Commercial Diamond Districts

Unless you have years of experience in diamond buying, shopping in diamond districts, especially in New York City, is a surefire way to get ripped off. These diamond dealers are professionals at spotting your relative lack of experience and charming you out of money.

Scammers & Scallywags

Unfortunately, there are many of my colleagues who are more crooked and corrupt than a crime boss. These knaves spend their days hustling every last dime from you, therefore making it seem as if all jewelers have a propensity for dishonesty. I can assure you that not all jewelers are like that. As a future diamond connoisseur, you've got to be able to spot these criminals and avoid their traps.

Forged Certificates

Scheming retailers can be in cahoots with discreditable labs. These labs use acronyms that seem similar to those of respected labs. For example using IGA instead of GIA, or AGL instead of EGL. A consumer sees this and thinks that the certificate was issued by a legitimate lab.

By inspecting the security features of your gem's certificate, you can avoid this scam. The respected labs have watermarks, micro lines and other security features that are unique to that lab. Some certificates are laminated and, if it has been tampered with, the laminate covering will look a bit strange, especially at the corners.

Buying The 'Best' Of The Bunch

Some jewelers carry only 'Fair' and 'Good' cut diamonds because they are cheaper in inventory costs and turn over relatively quickly. The problem is, sometimes these retailers try to pass off a 'Good' cut diamond as a higher cut grade gem with an expensive price tag to match. They may deliberately place an inferior quality gem right next to one that is only of slightly better quality. In the flurry of slick sales talk and gibberish, you may think that you're getting a great deal by choosing the better looking rock at a great price. Sorry to disappoint you, but you're really only getting the best of a bad lot. Be smart. Always demand reputable certificates!

Little Technicalities

Government regulations mandate that retailers must report the Color and Clarity grades of their diamonds within one grade level of that actual stated on the gem's certificate. In other words, if a gem has a certified color grade of 'H', a retailer is only obligated to list it one level higher or lower than 'H.' Naturally, no jeweler is going to list the gem with a lower grade especially when they can legally list it at the higher 'G' level and potentially get more money for it.

Clueless Jewelers

If you ask the question, "What color grade is it?" and your jeweler doesn't know, then you should put the stone down and leave. Diamonds are certified under stringent conditions to very exacting standards. Your jeweler's uncertainty is not only a sign of unprofessionalism, but also a bit of potential trickery at work. A competent jeweler should have the necessary certificates on hand to verify every detail.

Okay, maybe he's having a bad day; let's give him a break. You can ask to verify the color with the in-house Master Color Set and judge the color for yourself. Every jeweler has one, so if your jeweler is still hesitant, then you should leave. He has just confirmed that he's really up to no good.

The 'Pretty Woman Moment'

In 1990, the movie *Pretty Woman* was the talk of Hollywood. In it, the beautiful Julia Roberts played a street walker who was swept off her feet by a handsome, rich debonair man played by Richard Gere. There's a scene in which Julia, dressed in the attire of a woman of questionable repute, enters a high-end clothing store. Let's just say that the saleswoman was less than kind to her, until she realized that Julia could actually afford the merchandise in the store. I call this 'The Pretty Woman Moment.'

From time to time, 'Pretty Woman' moments occur and not just in jewelry stores. Slick retailers will sometimes artificially adjust the price of their wares based on the attire and persona of their customers and the amount they believe they can hustle out of clients. The sad thing is, if you have been deemed 'not of their caliber,' they'll just jack up the prices so that you'll walk away. If at any time during your diamond hunt you feel that you're caught in a 'Pretty Woman Moment,' it's best to leave that store. That retailer hasn't earned the right to be your jeweler.

'The Switcheroo'

This is the most devious and infamous of all the scams. Sadly, you can be duped several times throughout the tenure of your diamond ownership.

The Switcheroo starts innocently enough; boy sees a quality loose diamond, boy buys this diamond and pays for the jeweler to set it in a beautiful ring. Then boy walks away as pleased as punch. Unfortunately, a sneaky retailer has noticed that our Knight hasn't paid close attention to certain crucial details. The light bulb then goes off, a perfect set up for a Switcheroo!

The dishonest jeweler mounts *a* diamond according to our Knight's request, but he doesn't the mount *the* diamond our Knight bought. Instead, the jeweler sets an inferior quality gem and makes sure that all identifying elements (inscription numbers, noticeable inclusions, etc) are cleverly obscured by the setting. Since our Knight has locked into a contract for free cleaning and repairs, the retailer can repeat this switch as many times as he pleases.

A truly dishonest retailer can repeatedly sell the same diamond, simply by swapping out high priced, high quality gems for inferior ones every time the diamond must be cleaned, repaired or mounted. Mr. Sneaky X will keep his inventory stocked with mostly cheap, poorly cut diamonds, which cuts down on inventory costs, but he will keep selling the same high quality gem with a sky high price tag.

The easiest way to avoid this scam is to pay attention to details. Inspect your certificates. Do the inscription numbers match? Are the diamond's blemishes and inclusions identical to those listed on the diamond's Plot? Inspect your gem thoroughly every time it leaves your possession.

As an extra layer of precaution, you can have your loose diamond appraised independently immediately after purchasing, but before setting. Once the gem has been set, take it back to the same appraiser and ask him to give it a once over to verify that it is the same diamond he appraised a few weeks earlier. It helps if you take along the original appraisal report and the appraisals cost is a small price to pay for peace of mind.

'The False Sale'

Everybody loves a sale. Somehow that magic word brings out our innermost shopping urges. We believe that we're savvy consumers and feel like Kings and Queens of the Coupon whenever we leave a store with a ton of items and cash left to burn. Retailers know this and they take full advantage of it.

'The False Sale' is a common trick in all areas of commerce. It's true that a retailer may genuinely wish to move his inventory faster and will advertise a 'Blow Out' sale. However the Sneaks among them think of ways to extract more money from unsuspecting consumers. Some retailers artificially mark items at a higher value, then advertise the discounts in such a way, that the price works out to be the same as it was originally.

For example, our friend at Sneaky X Jewelry has a diamond priced at $2000. He may desperately want to sell it because it has been sitting in his store for a few weeks. Sneaky X is planning a sale. Just before the event, he increases the price of diamond to $4000, and then advertises a 50% discount on it.

Unsuspecting consumers see that a $4000 diamond now costs $2000 and thank their lucky stars that they've scored such a deal. The problem, however, is that the diamond was always being sold at $2000. The 'False Sale' was just a ploy to get people to buy a diamond that would've otherwise remained unsold.

This scam can also be called the 'Never-ending Liquidation' or 'Going out of Business Sale.' The retailer has been perpetually liquidating his business for the last 20 years, all while expanding his showroom and display counters. Just as in the case of the 'False Sale', it's all a ploy to get you to think that you're getting a great deal on a diamond.

Overweight Price Tags

This scam is the same as the 'False Sale' scam but without the 'Sale' sign. Dishonest retailers will artificially keep prices high in order to squeeze more money out of consumers. Some unsuspecting consumers will pay the inflated prices without any negotiations, while those who have been bitten by the bargain hunting bug will try to haggle. You may think that you're getting a great deal, but you've only managed to successfully haggle the price of the gem down to its original amount.

'Blue-White Diamonds'

I know you're not falling for that one! Blue-white diamonds? There's no such thing! The retailer is trying to pass off a highly fluorescent diamond as a perfect gem. It's like a car salesman telling you that the huge dent in your new car makes it sleeker and more appealing.

Only listing the Total Carat Weight (TCW)

Listing the Total Carat Weight (TCW) and not the weight of the center stone makes it hard to truly compare prices. A retailer may show you a piece that has a larger Total Carat Weight, but in reality, this is the total Carat Weight of many tiny, low quality stones. You may be tricked into believing that you're buying a large, high quality piece, when in fact, he's selling you a collection of inferior stones. Always know the carat weight of the center stone as this is always the most valuable of the group of stones in the piece. This will help you to make a better price comparison when deciding between several pieces.

Embellishments

Sometimes a retailer will try to pass off a low quality diamond that has been significantly treated and cosmetically enhanced as a higher quality diamond. If you fall for this scam, you are paying more for the 'Illusion of Perfection' than the actual value of the gem. Getting reputable certificates that list all the treatments that a stone has undergone will eliminate your chances of getting duped.

Bait and Switch

After searching online or in the local newspaper, you may have come across a diamond advertised that's perfect in both beauty and price. A quick call to the store and the sales person has assured you that the gem is immediately available. Delighted, you rush at break-neck speed to get to the store, only to discover that the gem is already sold. The retailer is so distraught about your missed opportunity that he offers other pricier options as a means of compensation. Sound familiar?

This is the old 'Bait and Switch.' Retailers are only interested in getting you into the store, and, through the miracle of some cockamamie story about a mix up in inventory, your chosen gem is suddenly out-of-stock. That gem was probably sold 20 years ago, but the retailer will still advertise it in the Sunday paper in the hopes of reeling you in.

"It's Guaranteed With A Deposit."

You are about to buy a gem but you still have some doubts. That's understandable; it is a large investment and it can be devastating if things go awry. Being the smart diamond connoisseur that you are, you want to get the gem appraised before committing and you know that in-house appraisals are a big No-No. After much debate, the jeweler offers up this compromise, "Take the gem and get it appraised but you have to leave a 50% deposit, just as a security measure." Sounds reasonable, right?

If you answered 'Yes', tsk, tsk. The retailer knows that he's about to sell you something that's a lemon, so he's willing to take half the money before you find out that it actually is! The deposit will be non-refundable and when you return with your new lemon to reclaim your money, the retailer will simply point to the fine-print and offer to give you another diamond in exchange. Eventually, you may be caught in a constant diamond swap, exchanging inferior stones for other inferior stones.

The Lowballers

Sometimes, it is the appraisers who are dishonest. Sneaky appraisers may tell you that your stone is worth a bag of nickels. Angry and frustrated, you march back to the jeweler and raise all hell to get back your money. He'll comply and sit baffled, wondering what went wrong. Although you may have your cash in hand, you're still left with a dilemma, where to go to get a diamond?

Suddenly, you remember a nice jewelry store a few blocks away that was recommended by the nice appraiser who warned you about your 'worthless' diamond. However, unbeknownst to you, both the new store and the appraiser are in cahoots. You have just given up a high quality diamond for a high priced dud from a new store.

Chapter 13 – Gift Ideas for Your Loved Ones

It can be intimidating if you're buying diamonds for your loved one. So far we've discussed what to look for in a diamond, but how do you shop for a piece that will overwhelm her with ecstatic exuberance?

Does she like Rounds or Lily diamonds? Fancy cuts?

Before you start tearing out your hair, wondering what to get her, let's talk about ways to suss out what she likes most. Think of it as Diamond Spying 101.

How to Buy Diamonds for Women

She's the 'Apple of your Eye,' the one that stole your heart. Every little thing about her is beyond perfect and you're already looking forward to the day when you two will argue over who spoils the grandkids more.

Whether you're working up the courage to pop the big question or just giving her a little token to brighten her day, buying jewelry for your Lady Love can be daunting. You're not quite sure what to get, or whether she'll love it.

Here are a few little pointers to help you navigate the waters of buying diamonds for your *belle femme*.

Know her Personality

It wouldn't really be much of a relationship if you guys didn't know each other well! Is she a happy-go lucky gal or super disciplined and organized? Does she love kicking it old school, or does she own every high tech gizmo before it has hit the general market? Is she prone to girly giggles or is she a tomboy at heart? Knowing who she is deep down can spare you the look of disappointment or confusion when she opens up her new present.

If your Love is super organized and disciplined, she may lean more towards pieces that are traditional or have clean lines like Rounds or Emeralds. In this case ask yourself, what would Grace Kelly or Jackie Onassis do? If she loves Humphrey Bogart movies and still rocks her grandma's hair brooch, then she'll melt for more antique gems. Rose cut, Fancy Colored diamonds are your best bet. A girly girl may find Lily diamonds cute, but Round and Princess cuts are good options as well.

A diamond has to not only wow the person receiving it, but also be a reflection of his/her personality.

Look Through Her Jewelry Box

To have an idea of what she likes, you can draw inspiration from what she already has. Doing so may help you to avoid the moment being ruined by an ill-fitting ring. But don't just watch the box as she's bound to have a 'polite stash.' These are jewelry pieces that she isn't too fond of and wears them on occasion. If you really want your gift to evoke happy squeals, look at what she wears most. Every girl has a few pieces that she'll throw on every chance she gets.

Go Shopping With Her

Suck it up and go shopping with her. For some men this can be a torture; you'd probably rather gouge out your toenails than spend a beautiful Saturday in some girly store, but do it for your Love. Think of it as a covert mission from some spy movie.

Don't complain, cop an attitude or sigh endlessly, since this sabotages the whole mission the nanosecond she senses that you're uncomfortable. If this happens, the day will end in a petty argument and you would've learned nothing.

Remember that you are trying to gather as much information as possible. Browsing through a few jewelry counters with her and judging her reaction to a few pieces, whether or not they're rings, is another great way to do so. But be subtle! Women are clever creatures and they will pick up your hidden agenda long before you can gather all your Intel.

Being sneaky while asking around can be tricky. Her close friends, her Mom or even her siblings can be great sources of information.

Stick With The Originals

For women, quality matters far more than quantity. It's better to buy her a small, high quality authentic piece than a huge, chunky one of lesser value, or even a fake.

Listen to Your Love

If she likes something, she will drop hints. Sometimes they'll be silent bombers, other times she'll shout it from the mountain top. The trick is learning how to recognize these hints; they can be longing looks at a De Beer's commercial or a fleeting compliment about some stranger's earrings. Do you see fashion or wedding magazines lying around a lot more than usual? If she's hearing wedding bells, she'll start casually shopping around.

Make it a Surprise

Everybody loves surprises. Fact! Surprising your Love with any gift means so much more than you can ever imagine, so take the time to plan the event. Think of all the details; will it be a romantic surprise or one designed to be light hearted and fun?

Surprises build a deeper emotional connection because she will really appreciate the time and effort that you've put into planning the whole event. It doesn't have to be expensive, but it must be unexpected. You want her to fall into a hysteric fit of girly giggles with teary streaks of makeup on her face as these are moments that she will remember most.

How To Buy Diamonds For Men

Now Ladies, you too must shell out for your Knight-In-Shining-Armor. After all, everybody loves feeling appreciated. You too will be engaged in a covert mission and you'll need lots of Intel to pull off the impossible.

Think of yourself as the female James Bond. - My name is Bond...Jane Bond. Your mission? To gather Intel on your hubby's jewelry tastes.

Know Your Man

Is he the cool sophisticated type, or more footloose and fancy free? Does he ooze swagger and sex appeal, or is he more the rugged Tarzan type? Remember this is his gift, so get something that *he* will adore, even if it's a big toe-shaped diamond ring. The gift must speak to his personality.

Go Shopping With Him

Go shopping with *him*. Watch what *he* picks out for *himself*. Suss out what *he* likes. Your mission is to observe, not to partake.

His Jewelry Box

Most guys have a few sticks of gum and the macaroni necklace that they made in kindergarten in their jewelry box, so it will be a little tricky to gather Intel there. A great place to start is to watch his watch. Every guy wears a watch and most will try to get one that reflects his sense of style.

Does he have cufflinks or rings? Take note of those too. Does he like his jewelry chunky or flashy? Walk by a few watch display counters with him and observe which ones leave him starry eyed.

Watch His Dream Car

A guy's dream car can tell you a ton about his likes and dislikes. Does he drool over the 2013 Aston Martin Vanquish? Or is he super old school? A 1964 Shelby Cobra perhaps?

If he's a Vanquish guy, then he's a flashy guy. Go for the cuts that maximize Brilliance and Fire. However, Mr. Old School prides himself on the classics. The clean, simple, sophisticated lines of an Emerald or an Asscher may pique his interest more than flashier cuts.

Do A Little Data Mining

Guys tend to drop hints about high tech gadgets and cars, but jewelry? That's tricky. You may have to dig a little for some information. Ask a close friend or watch him as he browses through a catalog, but please don't hand him a frilly, girly one. If you're lucky, your Honey will drop a hint or two.

He Likes Surprises Too

We all love surprises, so surprise your Knight with his gift. Plan the gift giving event to match his personality. If he's a laid back kind of guy, set a relaxed mood. If he's a flashy guy, then an event with lots of fanfare and attention will suit him well. Do something *he* enjoys. Remember, this is his moment and you want to leave him speechless.

Chapter 14 – I've Got My Diamond, Now What?

Congratulations! After carefully stalking your prey, sneaking up on diamonds in showroom cases, locking horns with retailers and cleverly side-swiping scallywags, you have successfully bagged your quarry. You've marched home in victory and presented your prize to adoring fans and now you are smiling satisfactorily every time you hear your Sweetie gush over the new accessory. Great job!

So now what?

Are You Insured?

Don't assume for a second that the shine of your seemingly indestructible diamond collection has not caught someone else's eye. In case the Devil has indeed found work for a few idle hands or some Ocean's Eleven wannabes want to pull off a home heist, you'll need protection.

If the ruffians somehow manage to outsmart the alarm system and outmaneuver 'Killer' the Chihuahua, then your next best bet is diamond insurance. Home or Renter's insurance only pays if the unthinkable happens in your home. A foot beyond the fence and you're on your own! In such a case, opting for personal property insurance can safeguard your beauties whether at home or away.

While most insurance companies offer three main policies which cover your jewelry collection, there are variations for each policy, the details of which can only be determined by you and your insurance provider.

Replacement Value Policy (RV)

In this policy, your collection is insured for an amount agreed upon at the time the policy is drafted and signed. This amount may is usually enough to replace the item, even if its value has appreciated over time.

Think of it this way. Twenty years ago you bought a diamond ring for $1000 and after years of effort, the bandits finally outsmarted 'Killer.' After crying and giving 'Killer' a treat for his valiant efforts against the scoundrels, you find a similar ring valued at $11,000.

Your friends at the insurance company will pay you the full $11,000 to replace your ring.

This is the most popular insurance policy among jewelry owners, but it comes with higher premiums in order to compensate for general appreciation in the price of diamonds, gems and precious metals. While the payment of the premiums may be a bit of a drag, if the worse happens, you'll still be smiling.

Actual Cash Value Policy (ACV)

You will be reimbursed for your misplaced or stolen collection at market value less depreciation. In other words, the underwriter takes into account not only the value of your gem, but also the price you could sell it for if you had the option of selling. I'll break it down with this scenario.

Your gem was appraised at a value of $10,000 and you feel happier than a kid on Christmas. However, in today's lousy economy people tend not to spend big on high price items like diamonds. As such, you can only expect to sell your rock at a measly $2000. Your diamond has depreciated by a whopping $8000. Your insurance friends will only cover up to $2000, leaving you grumpier than the Grinch.

Even in fantastic economic conditions, the insurance company will take into account that your ring has endured X years of bumps and scratches. As such, they will find a dollar value for all those years of wear and subtract this value from your original $10,000. Either way, you'll still be grumpy.

Agreed Value Policy (AV)

This process involves lengthy discussions between the owner and the underwriter about the reimbursement value. Both parties determine a set value, which may be higher or lower than the actual value of the gem, at the time of policy creation. In the event of an incident, the collection is reimbursed for that agreed amount only, regardless of whether or not it's enough to replace your jewelry.

Lengthy debates with the underwriter are quite normal, as both parties have different goals in mind. While you are trying to get the maximum amount for your gem, your insurance friends are trying not to pay too much.

It's wise to work out the exact terms of your policy before you buy, even if it means annoying your insurance representative every 20 seconds. It's better to know what you're getting into ahead of time than being surprised when disaster strikes.

Trying to pick up the pieces after such an event is traumatic enough without the added feeling of being bamboozled by your insurance company.

The amount of coverage that you'll get from your chosen policy depends entirely on your needs, the amount that you are most comfortable paying, and the terms agreed upon with your policy provider. In any case, it is always a good option to have this added layer of protection should the worse occur.

Diamond Care Tips

Guys keep their cars in prime condition. There's the weekend morning ritual, washing with special detergent, vacuuming, keeping the glass spotless, spit-shining the tires and the Mr. Miyagi styled 'wax-on, wax-off' with a baby soft cloth.

Consider your diamond collection to also be worthy of as much care and devotion as a collector drooling over a rare Honus Wagner (1909 - 1911) baseball card.

Set up a maintenance schedule with your jeweler. Jewelry, just like cars, needs a professional's touch every now and again to repair broken prongs and the like.

Diamonds are not as indestructible as Superman. Under no circumstance should you do heavy jobs like repaving the driveway while still wearing your 5 carat Princess cut. If it's more intense than washing a few lightly soiled dishes, take the rock off!

Diamonds are tough little things, so never store them together or even with other jewelry pieces as some damage is bound to occur. Each item in your collection should have its own cushioned little bed and be as sheltered as a fragile little egg.

If you don't wear your Bling very often, keep them tucked away in a fireproof safe. You've spent quite a bit for your collection, so give aspiring Ocean's Eleven crooks and bad luck fairies a challenge to get to it.

Just as you need a bath, so too does your diamond. Give it a quick wash with warm, soapy water and brush gently with little Timmy's toothbrush. If your rock is still not at its best, a quickie with some ammonia-based window cleaner works too. Afterwards, rinse thoroughly with water and wipe gently with a soft, lint-free cloth. But if your gem has been fracture filled, then ammonia-based window cleaner should be avoided.

When all else fails, a dip in an ultrasonic cleaner will solve all problems.

These tips will ensure that your diamonds maintain their brilliance and shine for years to come.

PART 3 - FROM THE LABORATORY OF VICTOR FRANKENSTEIN

If the prospect of selling an arm, a leg or even your first born child for a Princess cut seems a bit too much, then consider the alternatives. As is commonplace in modern society, 'Anything of value is always worth copying' and diamonds are a prime example.

After almost 120 years, humanity has finally perfected the art of Frankenstein diamonds that have all the allure and beauty of the Natural thing without the high price tag. Consumers now have numerous types of diamonds to choose from. Whether your interest is piqued by Fancy Color Gems, Synthetics or Simulated stones, lab brainiacs have created mesmerizing pieces to satisfy every need. Indeed, the types of diamonds being offered to John and Jane Q. Public are as varied as Forrest Gump's box of chocolates, but savvy diamond connoisseurs know exactly what's in the box.

Welcome to Part 3, a detailed look at lab-created diamonds and Diamond Simulants.

Chapter 15 – Synthetic Diamonds

Mother Nature will not be rushed. She takes her own sweet time to make her awe-inspiring creations. Humans, on the other hand, are busy creatures and we hate waiting. It's no surprise that we have developed a way to speed up the process of creating diamonds. Instead of waiting millions of years for some random, extinct volcano to spit out the next *Hope Diamond*, scientists have mastered the art of making diamonds in days.

Whether you prefer the term Synthetic, Man-made, Imitation, lab-grown, Cultivated or Cultured, they all refer to a class of diamonds conjured up by brilliant men and women clad in lab coats, safety goggles and pocket protectors. Recently, the industry has started to move away from the term 'Synthetic' as it leaves a dirty after-taste when uttered from the mouth of the consumer.

Which would you rather say, 'I bought a pair of Synthetic diamond earrings' or 'I bought a pair of Lab created diamond earrings?'

What are Synthetic Diamonds?

Since the 1870s, lab junkies have been obsessed with creating a cheap, high quality version of the beloved diamond. Whether this quest was motivated by the pursuit of scientific knowledge or a way to pull off the next brilliant high-end scam, I cannot say.

The push to create the perfect Synthetic began in earnest during WWII by the USA, Sweden and Russia (then known as the Soviet Union). In 1955, more than a decade after the war, scientists at the GE Research Laboratory in New York reported the successful synthesis of a diamond using their newly invented machine, the Diamond Press.

Of course, this stone was unworthy of the touch of a seasoned diamond cutter's expert blade, but continuous refinement of the process has, over the years, resulted in modern eco-diamonds that rival Mother Nature's version.

It is unlikely that you'll find any of these lab-created stones in many of the up-market jewelry stores, as most high-end retailers don't want to risk eroding their brand name.

How Synthetics Are Made

To date, Dr. Frankenstein has used four methods to bring life to his creation, but only the first two are employed on a commercial scale:

High-Temperature, High-Pressure (HTHP)

Graphite powder and a metal plug are placed at the top of a capsule while a tiny piece of synthetic diamond is inserted at the bottom. The capsule is then sealed, pressurized and heated. When a critical point is reached, the graphite melts and dissolves into the molten metal, which then makes its way to the bottom of the capsule.

A temperature difference between the two ends of the capsule encourages precipitation of the molten carbon onto the tiny slither of synthetic diamond at the bottom. If the reaction is maintained for a long time, a large gem will eventually be formed. HTHP experiments mimic how diamonds are formed under the earth's surface.

Low Pressure Chemical Vapor Deposition (LPCVD)

Diamonds aren't only formed underground; they also occur in space. In the vacuum of space no-one can hear you scream and the probability of achieving high pressure is virtually non-existent. It may sound like a scene from a Star Trek episode, but if you want diamonds in space, you've got to make some *plasma*.

In Physics, the term **Plasma** refers to any heated gas that has electrically charged particles floating within it. When a gas is superheated to thousands of degrees, the atoms and molecules within it become electrically charged because their electrons are being knocked off. This in turn makes the molecules stick to each other, creating a kind of 'gas slurry.' It's not quite a gas or a liquid; it's both.

Creating plasma isn't an everyday occurrence as it's only formed under extreme conditions.

In LPCVD, methane gas is pressurized and heated until it forms plasma. The ionized particles within the plasma clump together, eventually forming larger crystals of diamond. At the start of the experiment, a tiny piece of diamond is usually placed in the reaction chamber to encourage precipitation of the newly formed diamond crystals.

This method results in higher quality gems, and, although it is a simpler set up than an HTHP experiment, it's not as widely used. This is due to the higher costs associated with LPCVD.

Diamonds from thin air? Now that's the stuff of legends!

Detonation Nano-Diamonds

Nano-diamonds can be created by detonating graphite powder in a metal capsule. The heat and pressure of the explosion creates the perfect HTHP conditions, leading to tiny diamond crystals being precipitated in the aftermath of detonation.

Countries like China and Russia use this method for large scale production of small pieces of diamonds which are used for industrial purposes.

Ultrasonic Treatment of Graphite

One set of researchers has found a way to convert the points of your HB No. 2 pencils into your new Princess cut engagement ring by blasting clumps of graphite with sound waves. Pretty cool, don't you think?

How it works is rather ingenious. Graphite powder is placed in a special liquid and the speaker volume is turned up. As the sound wave passes through, it creates alternating pockets of high and low density (bubbles) within the liquid. Any gas dissolved in the liquid tries to escape the sections of high density by seeping into the bubbles. Once the system reaches a critical point, the ultrasonic wave is stopped and all the bubbles simultaneously collapse, instantly creating the perfect HTHP conditions for diamond formation. The carbon atoms in the graphite immersed in the liquid snap into a formation that is similar to how atoms are arranged in a natural diamond.

Of course, this all occurs under precise laboratory conditions and only creates micro crystals of diamonds. The technique has no commercial application as further research is needed to optimize this methodology.

What To Look For In Your Lab-Created Diamond

Cultured Diamonds are not held with the same regard as Natural Diamonds, although both are chemically and physically equal. They are considered to be inferior to the natural ones and, as such, are expected to be cheaper. Since unscrupulous dealers can try to pass off Synthetics as Natural diamonds, it is important for budding diamond connoisseurs to know how to differentiate between the two.

Natural diamonds *may* be laser inscribed. This is usually done at the dealer's or owner's discretion, although I encourage my future diamond experts to get their gems imprinted. However, the law requires that all Cultured diamonds *must* be inscribed without prior consent of the dealer or owner.

Since Synthetics are created under precise lab conditions, they're usually 'too perfect.' It is rare to find a Synthetic with any flaws, whereas it's impossible to find a flawless Natural diamond. If a Cultured diamond actually contains flaws, these are usually minute pieces of metal that were trapped during the gem's creation. As such, Cultured diamonds tend to be magnetic, unlike their Au-Natural cousins.

The arrangement of the carbon atoms within Cultured diamonds varies slightly from that of Natural stones making them generally heavier than similarly sized Naturals.

Lastly, Synthetic and Natural diamonds react differently to UV light. Both stones will have Fluorescence, but a cultured gem tends to continue glowing up to ten seconds after the UV light source has been removed; a trait unheard of in Natural diamonds.

Chapter 16 – Simulated Diamonds

Not all man-made diamonds are created equal and, in the realm of diamonds, Simulated diamonds are in their own class. As a budding diamond connoisseur, you need to know the ins and outs of these stones in order to help you to make informed decisions when it comes to buying your own gems.

What are Simulated Diamonds?

Simulated diamonds are also man-made inventions, but unlike their synthetic cousins, Sims aren't composed of carbon. They're made up of oxides of silicon, aluminum, yttrium and zirconium (to name a few) and are designed to resemble natural diamonds.

There are several popular types of materials from which Sims can be produced:

Cubic Zirconia (CZ)

CZ pieces were used in the late 1970s by the Russians (formerly known as The Soviet Union) as part of laser experiments. In the 1980s, mass production of Cubic Zirconia jewelry began in earnest and today CZ is the most popular Simulated diamond.

It's manufactured using the Skull Crucible process perfected by scientists in the former Soviet Union. Zirconium oxide powder and a piece of Zirconium metal are gradually heated in special equipment using radio waves like those emitted when you blast Led Zeppelin's *Stairway to Heaven* (1976) from your speakers. When the mixture is cooled, the atoms within the molten powder line up in a manner similar to that of the atoms in diamonds. The newly formed, gem quality Cubic Zirconia crystals are then cut and set in jewelry pieces.

CZ diamonds mimic the light performance of real diamonds.

Moissanite

Since 1998, Moissanite has been used as jewelry under the trade name of 'Berzelian.' It's hard to believe but Moissanite's light properties surpass those of diamonds. These beauties out-shine Natural diamonds and have a Fire like none other. But alas, despite all this, their value is still far below that of their Au-Natural and Synthetic cousins.

The mineral was discovered by Dr. Moissan in 1893 at a meteorite crash site in the Diablo Canyon, New Mexico. Moissanite is made up of the elements silicon and carbon, and is more durable and heat-resistant than diamond. Since naturally occurring Moissanite is rare, most of the gems are manufactured using the HTHP method.

White Sapphire (Al_2O_3)

The word 'Sapphire' conjures up images of a beautiful, deep blue stone, but it may surprise you to know that sapphire actually comes in all colors of the rainbow. White Sapphire was the most popular Simulated diamond before the advent of Cubic Zirconia.

White Sapphire is really an oxide of Aluminum and is almost as hard and durable as diamonds. However, these beauties lack the Brilliance and shine of the real thing. The stone is mined from countries like Sri Lanka, Madagascar, Burma, Australia and Tanzania. Stones from Sri Lanka are also known as Ceylon White Sapphire.

White Sapphire has a place in the realm of the supernatural. In the Orient, it is believed that the stone brings good luck and fortune to the wearer.

Yttrium Aluminum Garnet (YAG)

YAG is an oxide of Aluminum and Yttrium and is also referred to as Diamonique. It is another great diamond alternative, often sold on home-shopping channels like QVC. They have many properties similar to diamonds, including clarity, durability and light performance but are noticeably heavier than similarly sized diamonds.

Simulated vs. Synthetics: What's the Difference?

Unfortunately, many published sources of information confuse the two and believe that Simulated and Synthetic diamonds are one and the same. They aren't!

Both Synthetic and Natural Diamonds are made of the same material - carbon. When graphite, which only consists of carbon atoms, is exposed to high temperature and high pressure, Synthetic diamonds are created. In comparison to Natural diamonds, Synthetics only have very few differences in their properties like magnetism and lingering Fluorescence. These differences arise from the method by which synthetics are created and aren't a feature of the type of material that they are composed of.

On the other hand, Simulated Diamonds are not made of carbon at all! Simulated diamonds have vastly different properties when compared to Natural diamonds, and as such, a diamond connoisseur like you can easily spot the difference between the two.

How to Spot a Simulated Diamond a Mile Away

When purchasing Natural diamonds, it's important to know the tell tale signs of Sims so that you don't end up dropping boatloads of cash on something that carries no real value. Simulated diamonds are extremely easy to spot if you know what to look for.

Abbreviations

If you happen to be buying a mounted diamond, be on the lookout for the letters 'CZ,' 'YAG' or any such inscription that could be an abbreviation of known materials used to make Simulated diamonds. By law, manufacturers of these types of stones are required to indicate on the gem the material from which it is made.

Background Setting

It is rather pointless to set a Simulated diamond in an expensive mount made of Gold or Platinum. Sims are usually set in cheaper metals like silver, so this is another telltale sign that the piece you're looking at is probably a Simulated diamond.

Magnifying Glasses

Simulated diamonds make great magnifying glasses too. By placing the gem against any printed material, you can tell whether or not it's a Sim. Real diamonds, whether Synthetic or Natural, have tons of Brilliance and Fire. The light within bounces around so much that it's impossible to see straight through the gem to read anything on the printed page.

A Simulated diamond however, lacks the Light Performance of a real diamond. If you can easily read the fine print on your warranty with the Sim that the dealer is about to sell you, then you know that this is a store where you shouldn't be spending your hard earned money.

The Breathalyzer

Doing the Breath test with or without a Tic Tac is an easy way to spot Sims. Blowing on the fake diamond, as you would when trying to fog up a mirror, results in a foggy stone whereas a real diamond would remain as clear as day.

Too Good To Be True

Paying rock bottom prices for a gem that is absolutely flawless is impossible. Almost all Natural diamonds have blemishes and inclusions when viewed under magnification.

A stone that is perfect and costs less than a few hundred thousand dollars is a stone that was cooked up by a lab technician.

The Black Light Show

All real diamonds, whether Synthetic or Natural, will glow under UV light, even to a small degree. Simulated diamonds on the other hand, are not made up of carbon and as such, have no Fluorescence at all.

Synthetic, Simulated or Au-Natural - Which Do You Prefer?

Comparing the three is like comparing Gala Apples, Gala Supreme Apples and Pineapples; they may sound like the same thing, but in reality, they are all in completely separate baseball leagues.

Simulated Diamonds are the pineapples of the bunch and your propensity for these stones really depends on what you want from your jewelry. If you're a connoisseur on a Soda budget and you only want the illusion of a diamond, then Sims are for you especially if you don't expect your gem to undergo intense scrutiny, or think that your jewelry piece will be a lasting family heirloom. In this case, you're perfectly happy with creating the Illusion of Grandeur and not shelling out too much for it.

If you or your loved one is a die-hard Recessionisto/Recessionista, then you will be content with the Gala Supreme Apples of the diamond world. Synthetic diamonds pack all the allure and charm of a Natural diamond at a fraction of the cost and are eco-friendly. It's difficult to tell the difference between the two, unless your gem is being scrutinized by the Bionic Woman or the Six Million Dollar Man.

For the purists and the picky, nothing but the real thing will do. You will never be content with 'Grucci,' 'Plada' or anything other than the original. Going Au-Natural will set you back financially quite a bit, but you'll have a valuable family heirloom for generations to come.

Regardless of which gem you choose, the only important factor is the happiness of the Love of your Life. If your relationship is built of sterner stuff, then a shiny Mantle piece is only a small token of what you truly mean to each other.

CONCLUSION – A LESSON WELL LEARNED

You have learned the fundamentals of the 6Cs, navigated dangerous waters filled with scammers and scallywags and taken a glimpse into the world of diamond alternatives. The diamond realm is vast, beautiful, and complex, requiring a few years of intense research to become a true expert. But by now you have garnered enough information to morph into a budding diamond aficionado.

With a few helpful pointers and tips, you can now make informed decisions on your next diamond expedition and bag a quarry worthy of a flood of accolades.

All that's left to say is Good Luck and Happy Diamonding!

Printed in Great Britain
by Amazon.co.uk, Ltd.,
Marston Gate.